WITHDRAWN FROM
KENT STATE UNIVERSITY LIBRARIES

Libraries and Librarianship in the Muslim World

Series Editors
Mumtaz A. Anwar
Abbas S. Tashkandy

Information Services in Muslim Countries

An Annotated Bibliography of Expert Studies and Reports on Library, Information and Archive Services

Mumtaz A. Anwar

Mansell Publishing Limited
London and New York

First published 1985 by Mansell Publishing Limited
(A subsidiary of The H. W. Wilson Company)
6 All Saints Street, London N1 9RL, England
950 University Avenue, Bronx, New York 10452, USA

©Mumtaz A. Anwar 1985

All rights reserved. No part of this publication may be reproduced or transmitted in any form or by any means, electronic or mechanical, including photocopy, recording or any information storage or retrieval system, without permission in writing from the publishers or their appointed agents.

British Library Cataloguing in Publication Data

Anwar, Mumtaz, A.
   Information services in Muslim countries : an annotated bibliography of expert studies and reports on library, information and archive services.—(Libraries and librarianship in the Muslim world)
   1. Information services—Islamic countries—Bibliography
   I. Title II. Series
   016.0255′2′0917671   Z64.5.18

ISBN 0-7201-1781-X

Library of Congress Cataloging in Publication Data

Anwar, Mumtaz A.
   Information services in Muslim countries.

   (Libraries and librarianship in the Muslim world)
   Bibliography: p.
   Includes indexes.
   1. Information services—Islamic countries—Bibliography. 2. Libraries—Islamic countries—Bibliography. 3. Archives—Islamic countries—Bibliography. I. Title. II. Series.
Z674.5.I74A59 1985   020′.917671   85-17211
ISBN 0-7201-1781-X

Typeset by Spire Print Services Ltd., Salisbury, Wiltshire
Printed in Great Britain by Henry Ling Limited, Dorchester, bound by Green Street Bindery, Oxford

Contents

Preface	vi
Introduction	viii
The International Role of Library Consultants	
E. R. Dyer and *P. Layzell Ward*	1
On the Librarianship of Poverty	
K. J. Mchombu	13
The Bibliography	25
Joint Author Index	123
Subject Index	125
Title Index	135

Preface

There is a general lack of bibliographical information on library and information services in the Muslim world. The idea for the present work developed out of a search for material on national libraries in Muslim countries. A number of references consisted of consultant reports. Contents of these documents, in general, do not find their way into the professional literature. It was felt that a listing of such reports should provide a good working tool to researchers interested in the area. As the number of citations started increasing the search was widened to check additional sources and to cover all aspects of library and information service. It is hoped that this work will help fill part of the bibliographical gap.

All possible sources including bibliographies, books, dissertations, and journal articles were consulted to find out published and unpublished reports. *Unesco bulletin for libraries* and the *Unesco list of documents and publications* (ULDP) were thoroughly checked. The coverage of *ULDP* starts from 1977. Listing of earlier Unesco reports is not complete. Automated database at the U.S. Agency for International Development was searched. This database, going back to 1974, includes reports of U.S. origin. The coverage of American reports prepared before 1974 is sketchy. Beverly Brewster's 'An analysis of American overseas library technical asssistance, 1940-1970' (Ph.D. dissertation, University of Pittsburgh, 1974) was also checked. Reports of committees appointed by governments of various countries have been excluded. Citations for some reports could not be located in original form. In such cases citations of summaries or published articles, when available, were included. Some of these items are: Parker's 'Proposals for library development in the Hashemite Kingdom of Jordan' (item 240), Sharify's *The Pahlavi National Library of the future* (item 289), and

Thompson's 'Library mission to Kuwait' (item 305). The year 1984 is only partially covered. In spite of extensive search, this bibliography makes no claims to completeness.

The bibliography is preceded by two articles. E. R. Dyer and P. Layzell Ward in 'The international role of the library consultant' discuss the ramifications of the role of an extranational library consultant in the third world. The view projected by the authors is a western one. 'On the librarianship of poverty' by K. J. Mchombu deals with the environment in which information services as seen by the foreign experts are to prosper. This piece of writing provides a third world view which is not widely understood and appreciated by the extranational consultants. These articles taken together provide a useful background for the bibliography.

The entries are arranged alphabetically under author, the first in case there are more than one and under title if no author was mentioned—all in one sequence. Separate indexes for joint authors, subjects and titles are provided. Citation for the report is followed by annotation and/or keywords when available. The last segment is the document number for the report. Annotations and keywords have been reproduced from the *Unesco list of documents and publications* and from the U.S.A.I.D. automated database printout with permission.

Access to these reports, in general, is limited. American reports, if available, can be acquired from A.I.D. Document and Information Handling Facility, 7222 47th Street, Chevy Chase, MD 20815, U.S.A. Most of the Unesco reports when submitted are marked 'Restricted'. In many cases, however, restriction is removed after some years. Requests for these reports may be addressed to Reports Division (CPX), Unesco, 7 place de Fontenoy, 75700 Paris, France. A good collection of reports is available in the International Library Information Center, Graduate School of Library and Information Sciences, University of Pittsburgh, Pittsburgh, U.S.A.

I am grateful to Unesco and to U.S.A.I.D. for permitting me to reproduce annotations of expert reports from *ULDP* and the A.I.D. automated database.

Introduction

Information services, primitive or modern, good or bad, reflect the requirements and resources of a particular social group. These services can be a little forward or a little backward but the gap cannot be too wide. Their growth and prosperity depends on the urgency of the needs of a particular group and financial resources available to it. In other words, information and library services are part of the social environment and their growth is governed by the soil in which their roots are found. It is quite possible that a developing country may have excellent special libraries, whereas public libraries may be non-existent for 80 per cent of its population. Should one, out of enthusiasm or sympathy, try to intervene and provide library service for this unprivileged group by using standards followed by developed countries? Or, should one analyze and try to understand the situation as it exists and provide services, not necessarily traditional library services, which relate to the actual needs of this group and which can be gainfully used by it.

The literature presented in this bibliography is of a very special type. It is the result of an expressed interest, local or foreign, in accelerating the growth of library and information services in Muslim countries as part of the third world. Before taking a look at this body of literature, a brief discussion of the position of libraries and information services in these countries seems to be in order.

Most of the Muslim countries, politically speaking, have had a similar experience—a long pre-colonial independent past, a period of political, commercial and cultural domination by a foreign country, and a comparatively short period of independence. Each of these segments had its own distinct information needs and, in turn, developed information services to fulfil these needs.

During the pre-industrial and pre-colonial period Muslim countries developed adequate information services relevant to their needs at that time. Information, both oral and written, was being generated and utilized in all aspects of life. Availability of appropriate information created a socio-economic system which continued to progress, prosper and remain self-sufficient for centuries. During this period, there were reasonably developed library services, from private collections to academic, public and court libraries. Along with repositories of written records, oral transmission of historical and cultural information developed into a specialized skill practised by individuals in each community.

Foreign political domination shifted the administrative and financial support from the existing institutions to those established and required by the colonial powers. This shift retarded the growth of libraries, changed them from active resources to stagnant collections of manuscripts and eventually caused their dispersal in and outside each country. However, at the same time a new breed of libraries developed: those in newly established academic and research institutions; those set up for government functionaries; and circulating or subscription libraries for 'gentlemen'. A fairly common characteristic was that most of these libraries were isolated pockets of primarily foreign information resources which did not emerge from and did not cater to the needs of the local population.[1]

Freedom from colonial rule brought with it a strong urge for rapid growth. Swift change, however, needed resources and services that were not available locally. At this juncture former colonial powers assumed the role of aid-giving countries. In the eyes of local authorities development was seen as high doses of planned growth in all fields of national life. The question whether these doses were appropriate or digestible was rarely discussed or explored in detail. The outcome of decades of planned development effort, in general, has been less than encouraging.

These developing Muslim countries at the present time are deficient in many ways. Economically and industrially backward (excepting of course the oil producing nations), they largely depend on foreign raw materials and finished goods and are short of foreign exchange. Their populations are growing fast, but they are short in food production. Most of their people are uneducated and their contribution to world information output is negligible. Although more can be added to this catalogue of poverty, we should remember, however, that any prescription to remove these deficiencies must be preceded by a careful diagnosis and should take into consideration the local temperament and resources.

x   *Introduction*

Modern librarianship as it is understood today was introduced into the Muslim world mainly after World War II. Foreign interest in library development came from aid-giving countries, Unesco, and private foundations. More often than not, this interest brought with it the services of experts and consultants who worked either on projects funded by the aid-giving agencies or studied and reported on a particular situation. There is a reasonable amount of such literature for Muslim countries, and what contribution these studies have made is a subject in its own right. Unfortunately, followup and evaluative studies are not often undertaken.

This bibliography consists of 338 reports sponsored by Unesco, aid-giving countries, private foundations and in many cases by the country concerned itself. Of the forty-five members of the Organization of the Islamic Conference (O.I.C.), three do not have a single entry: Brunei, Jibouti, and, quite understandably, Palestine. The number of reports for other countries varies considerably, from a minimum of one to a maximum of thirty. Do these figures in any way reflect a country's interest in its information services, its clout in Unesco, or its political importance in the eyes of aid-giving countries?

Number of Reports Per Country

Country	#	Country	#
Afghanistan	7	Malaysia	7
Algeria	10	Maldives	1
Bahrain	2	Mali	10
Bangladesh	7	Mauritania	7
Benin	9	Morocco	20
Bourkina Faso	7	Niger	7
Cameroon	11	Oman	2
Chad	4	Pakistan	12
Comoros	1	Qatar	6
Egypt	30	Saudi Arabia	9
Gabon	6	Senegal	19
Gambia	6	Sierra Leone	7
Guinea	4	Somalia	5
Guinea Bissau	1	Sudan	12
Indonesia	22	Syria	4
Iran	17	Tunisia	19
Iraq	12	Turkey	12
Jordan	8	Uganda	9
Kuwait	7	U.A.E.	3
Lebanon	11	Yemen, A.R.	3
Libya	7	Yemen, P.D.R.	1

Almost three-quarters of the reports (73.7 per cent) are sponsored by Unesco, which over the years has had a changing role in library development. Beginning with a somewhat limited approach in the form

Introduction xi

of sponsoring seminars, conferences, pilot projects and fellowships, Unesco adopted a comprehensive approach with the concept of UNISIST (World Science Information System—1971) and NATIS (National Information System—1974). The number of reports after the adoption of UNISIST and NATIS seems steadily to have grown. The second major sponsor of expert studies is the United States (16.6 per cent). The pattern of American sponsored studies over the years, however, looks more like a flurry than a consistent and sustained interest in library development. The number of reports varies from year to year and seems to be influenced by shifting political interest followed by an increase or decrease in aid funds. A case in point is the number of studies on Egypt sponsored immediately following the Camp David agreement. The following table provides a yearly breakdown of the reports in the bibliography.

Yearly Breakdown of Reports

Year	Unesco	U.S.	Other	Total
1984	2	0	0	2
1983	13	1	0	14
1982	17	5	0	22
1981	16	6	0	22
1980	32	0	0	32
1979	17	0	2	19
1978	14	8	0	22
1977	29	3	1	33
1976	25	0	3	28
1975	19	0	2	21
1974	12	3	0	15
1973	13	1	2	16
1972	14	1	1	16
1971	2	0	0	2
1970	3	0	4	7
1969	3	0	0	3
1968	3	2	10	15
1967	0	2	0	2
1966	3	6	0	9
1965	4	6	0	10
1964	5	1	0	6
1963	1	3	2	6
1962	–	–	–	–
1961	1	0	0	1
1960	1	0	0	1
1959	0	1	1	2
1958	0	1	0	1
1957	0	0	1	1
1956	0	1	1	2

xii *Introduction*

Yearly Breakdown of Reports (*continued*)

Year	Unesco	U.S.	Other	Total
1955	0	1	0	1
1952	0	0	1	1
1942	0	0	1	1
1939	0	1	0	1
1916	0	0	1	1
No date	0	3	0	3
Total	249	56	33	338

Coverage of various areas of library and information services in these reports is not equally distributed. This unevenness indicates that a policy for an over-all development of library services in these countries does not exist.

National libraries are covered in twenty-five studies for fourteen (31.8 per cent) of the forty-four countries, with Palestine excluded. Egypt had four reports; Iran and Mauritania, three each; Indonesia, Pakistan, Somalia and Tunisia, two each; and one each for Benin, Cameroon, Gambia, Guinea, Iraq, Malaysia and Maldives. NATIS is also discussed in twenty-five reports covering nineteen (43.18 per cent) countries. Egypt, Indonesia, Iran, Iraq, Pakistan and Sudan each had two reports, with single reports for Afghanistan, Algeria, Benin, Bourkina Faso, Cameroon, Gabon, Jordan, Libya, Qatar, Senegal, Somalia, Tunisia and Uganda.

About half the Muslim countries do not publish national bibliographies, and those that are published are generally incomplete in coverage and issued late and irregularly. Important as national bibliographies are, they are the subject of only three reports for as many countries: Cameroon, Indonesia and Tunisia. Library networks are dealt with in two studies on Indonesia and one each on Malaysia and Senegal. It may be pointed out that in many cases one report covers several areas and is, therefore, mentioned under each.

Most Muslim countries, like other third world nations, suffer from what may be called a 'literacy' disease: high illiteracy is generally projected as a curse that must be eradicated at all costs. Following the clamour at international level, campaigns in many countries focus for a few weeks each year on 'educating' millions of adult illiterates then leaving them to lapse into their happy state of oral literacy. It is strange that instead of providing inexpensive essential information in oral form in cultures with strong oral traditions huge sums of money are spent by poor countries on adult literacy with no arrangements whatsoever to sustain it. The whole idea of alphabetic literacy being essential for socio-economic development is questionable.

Meaningful universal literacy has never been achieved in short periods of time or by teaching poor adult souls alone. It can only be achieved by compulsory primary education, emphasis on teaching children the use of information as a part of school textbooks and giving high priority to school and public libraries. An American child starts learning the use of a dictionary, and encyclopaedia, an index and a library catalogue from grade four,[2] whereas a third-world student may complete twelve years of study without hearing anything about these concepts.

School libraries, the backbone of universal literacy, are the subject of studies on five countries only: Kuwait, Libya, Mali, Morocco and Uganda. Rural libraries are the most neglected ones, covered in four reports on three countries: Benin, Indonesia and Pakistan. It is sad, indeed, to note that school and rural public libraries are totally neglected, whereas huge amounts of scarce financial resources are wasted on cosmetic adult literacy. This is one indication of lopsided development.

The scope, nature and size of these reports also varies widely. They range from royal dreams of national libraries (item 289) to brief down-to-earth proposals. Their impact on library development is difficult to evaluate.

Consultant reports, by their very nature, are elusive. Access to them, as a general rule, is restricted. Their implementation depends on the urgency of the project and the availability of continued financial assistance. Some have never been implemented. Others may actually have discouraged the host governments with unrealistic recommendations that included follow-up advisors, foreign scholarships for local librarians, expensive equipment, etc. As a result, library development may have been delayed by a decade or more. The Key report submitted in 1956 (item 183) has never seen the light of the day simply because of its financial implications for a newly independent and poor country which was faced with caring for millions of refugees.

One wishes all consultants' reports were written after careful consideration of the local needs and resources. The role of the consultant is crucial and is discussed in detail by Dyer and Ward in the following article. An important question is: Does the consultant have the time and flexibility to modify his experience to suit the needs of a situation that is usually totally different from that in his own country? In the second following article, 'On the librarianship of poverty', R. J. Mchombu describes the situation where the consultant can and needs to contribute. Whereas a number of studies have been made of 'culture' or 'role' shock as experienced by an extra-national consultant, the

xiv *Introduction*

other side of the coin has not been given any importance. There is an urgent need for an evaluative study of the success or failure of consultants' reports, and the reasons behind that success or failure.

References

1. Recommended for further study are Dora Lockyer's 'The provision of books and libraries by the East India Company in India, 1611–1858'. (Fellowship thesis, The Library Association, 1977) and Adolphe O. Amadi's *African libraries: Western tradition and colonial brainwashing* (Metuchen, N.J.: Scarecrow, 1981).
2. *Flying hoofs*, by Ira E. Aaron and others. Glenview, Ill.: Scott, Foresman, 1978, pp. 300, 409. (This is a grade four textbook).

The International Role of Library Consultants

E. R. Dyer and P. Layzell Ward

The Consultant's Role in Library Development

The purpose of this section is to provide a framework for the commentary which follows, concerning the exchange of ideas, suggestions and experiences among consultants and those who have received the advice of extra-national consultants. In keeping with the IFLA theme of 'Global Information Exchange: Librarianship in Developing Countries', the focus of this paper is squarely on the role of the extra-national consultant in the development of information services in those countries. Why this topic? The role of the extra-national consultants is an important topic for both consultant and receiver of such technical advice. Important because vast benefits may be derived from such a process as well as many problems that need to be overcome. The contributions of these consultants to the development of library services in many regions of the world are well known. However great these contributions are, there have been and continue to be many problems inherent in a process which superimposes the cultural mind set, technical expertise and varied experiences of individuals from one culture upon the national realities of another country. Problems do exist in this process, yet the problem can be minimized and the contributions and potential use can be maximized.

What is a Consultant?

Various definitions of a library consultant have appeared in the literature. James Lockwood in his article 'Involving Consultants in Library Change', adapted a definition of management engineer consultants to

© 1982 Academic Press Inc. (London) Limited

librarianship:

> A library consultant may be defined as an individual qualified by education, experience, technical ability, and temperament to advise or assist on a professional basis in identifying, defining and solving specific library problems involving the organization, planning, direction, control and operation of a library. The consultant serves the library as an impartial, objective advisor and is not an employee of its organization.[1]

The essential elements of this definition are professional abilities of the consultant coupled with the temperament of personal capability to advise, define or suggest solutions of library problems. Furthermore emphasis is placed upon the objectivity of the consultant as an outside impartial agent.

Some distinctions have been made between a consultant as one who works on a project from the conception to completion and a critic who intervenes at a specific point in a project. In practice these lines are not as defined and the critic and consultant can be considered as one role. Additionally some cynics have described consultants alternately as hired scapegoats, missionaries, change agents and occasionally peacemakers, depending of course on the viewpoint and the image of the project consultant. Indeed, while the formal definition of a consultant can be readily accepted, these latter roles are also a part of the consultant's role and may be included in the hidden agenda of both the employer and the consultant himself.

The descriptors applied to the consultant's role vary as a function of the expectations of the employer and the ability of the consultant to fulfil both stated and unstated objectives. Ultimately, success for both employer and consultant depends upon communications, definition and agreement on shared objectives, common perceptions of the problem, agreement as to preferred approaches to the problem and the parameters of the project. Among the obstacles to understanding is that of intercultural communications. Definitions of the problem identify cultural differences, such as space, time territoriality and social conventions as blocks which must be overcome or neutralized.[2] Additionally, the human contracts made by the consultant are brief, lacking both past and future as well as many factors at variance with the accepted mode of the consultant's culture. Take, for example, the space difference between American and Middle Easterner. The American prefers a substantial distance between himself and others in conversation. On the other hand when someone from the Middle East, wants to have an exchange of ideas, wants to accent a particular feeling in conversation, he tends to move closer and closer to his colleague. Without meaning to do so it is quite possible for the American to back away. Literally to back himself into a corner as the Middle Easterner moves forward to make his point. In the jockeying for culturally acceptable space, understanding of the content of the interaction may be lost or in the extreme, each may perceive a degree of hostility in the other where none exists. The consultant, like the traveller, is adrift in a new social structure, without links to past and future. The consultant meets contemporaries, those who share a community of time. The essence of the consultant's experience is that he and his colleague become 'consociates'—individuals who actually meet, share ideas and space as well as time.[3]

Knowing about a culture, values of time, space and priorities are important for successful interaction with other professionals. Some people never experience that often used phrase 'culture shock'. A strange culture can place many demands on the consultant, resulting in mounting pressure of fatigue, strangeness, overtaxed health and feelings of separateness and intellectual inability to react to new situations and needs of daily living. Some consultants, as well as the leisure travellers, never experience culture shock and are flexible enough in life style to be able to adapt more readily to new situations and to new patterns of interaction.

Situations that Lead to the Employment of Consultants

There are a variety of considerations that lead libraries, national planning agencies, universities, and international agencies to seek the services of a consultant. A classic consulting situation exists when 'desired expertise is lacking for significant portions of a project and when the period of required expertise is delineated'.[4] Domestically in the United States the single most common situation is that of facilities planning. Internationally, the motivating force is by and large the overall lack of trained librarians in developing countries and their interest in technical expertise. Sometimes, foreign aid or international agencies make funds available for special projects and they customarily include extranational consultants as part of a standard package along with equipment and long term training of nationals. Generally speaking the reasons for employing an outside consultant include technical expertise, specialized skills, fresh ideas, ability to focus on specific problems, objectivity and ability to exercise additional influence on decision makers.

Typical projects for consultants include long-range planning, local surveys, collection development, architectural considerations, automation, development of bibliographic systems, library education, development of specific types of libraries, establishment or improvement of national library services and their functions within the parent organization. Within these rather broad examples of consultant projects the functions of the consultants range from influencing funding or governing agencies towards a particular viewpoint, to mediating conflict within the existing system, providing a non-biased, non-political source of information, encouraging linkages and improving communications among professional reviewing current organization structures and recommending long-range plans for development. A perceived benefit of employing a consultant is that of providing funding credibility—the consultant with little vested interest supports for the world outside the library the need for additional resource allocation, increased budgets and staff requirements. Often however this is unrealistic since the range of the consultant's suggestions and ability to suggest improvements is limited by the hidden agenda of the employer and perhaps the financial interest of the consultant in being recommended for future employment and by the international organization. It may be difficult to satisfy the two masters—the host country and the international agency.

How are Consultants Found?

The process is neither scientific nor uniform and often comprises serendipity and the invisible college, instead of full information and adequate appraisal of a consultant's credentials. The majority of consultants are found through the invisible college, that person-to-person interaction of professionals, and the experts used by such agencies as Unesco, OAS, and CIDA. To use a personal example, last year I was contacted by the Instituto de Libro in Brazil to teach a course on school development. I had never to my knowledge met anyone from this organization nor applied for such a position. My name surfaced through this invisible network—someone I had met at a professional meeting several years earlier. Once it was determined that I could arrange my schedule to meet their needs I was hired. My credentials were sent only about two weeks before I arrived. While in Brazil I was asked to recommend people for future consulting positions and thus perpetuated the network I criticize. The whole situation points to the need for developing countries to have an adequate review process for consultants under consideration.

Another means of choosing professional consultants is through reputation and publications. Obviously, a person's publications reflect his or her interests and may demonstrate levels of competency. However, reputation is an intangible measure. For example, someone who has an excellent reputation in his native country, and who has become well regarded by the library establishment may not be flexible enough to adapt time honoured principles of one country to the experiences of a developing one. And in fact, this highly regarded consultant may offer pet solutions to library problems and may take the attitude that since this is how it is done in New York, London or Munich the same approaches are valid in Lima, Kingston, Addis Ababa and Cairo. Invariably employment of such a consultant, often one who has never been abroad before leads to disenchantment, frustration and failure to resolve adequately the problem at hand. Other sources of consultants are derived from advertisements by the consulting firms or individuals themselves.

Use of a single consultant as opposed to a team is another common initial problem faced by employers. A single consultant is most appropriately employed in such situations as course development, library education seminars and self-contained studies. In other words, where a specialist or expert's advice is needed for a specific limited period. One of the major difficulties encountered by the single consultant is the lack of peer support, the inability to communicate with other experts on locations and the need to operate alone. At times this problem can be alleviated by the use of consulting teams; thus providing the opportunity for diversification, interaction and additional input from both outside and inhouse sources. While both consultant and employer strive for the idea in the initial problem negotiation and establishing of understanding, subsequent problems that arise may ultimately be beyond both their control. Such factors as changes in government, policy, legislative barriers, political exigencies, bureaucratic status, staff changes and lack of clerical support or acts of God can be cited as examples of uncontrollable forces. In order to minimize these problems at least one local expert conversant with library politics and ministry of education procedures should be assigned to the consultant or consultants as a trouble shooter and liaison officer.

What are the Qualifications and Qualities of a Good Consultant?

The most important is the intangible asset of flexibility and cultural tolerance, precisely those qualities which cannot be evaluated by traditional means such as position or publications. The ideal consultant is culturally tolerant, is adaptable and able to understand the people with whom he will work, and possesses the ability to listen to in-house priorities and assess the capability of adapting to the new environment. While the consultant's technical expertise is essential, in specific situations it is often the generalist who can put together the various strands of librarianship and apply those ideas which best fit the problem at hand and bring together in a team effort the ideas of specialists.

Perhaps the best consultants are those judged to be 'mavericks' of the profession. Maverick is an Americanism that refers to the lone steers who shunned the herd, crossing the plains. Mavericks very often are on the cutting edge of change, not afraid to voice unpopular opinions and to defend positions that are at odds with the norm. High prestige from the library community may even be synonymous with rigidity and bias towards one system.

Lastly, consultants may be suggested or even mandated by such organizations as OAS or Unesco. Here much depends upon the political clout of the programme directors. The variance in the quality of consultants is great.

The current informal and formal structures are inadequate. An international clearing house could be established to form a data base of potential and active consultants, including curriculum vitae, language skills and availability. Organization to develop such a base would be, of course, IFLA. National associations might assume responsibility for development of a roster of consultants within their respective committees. For example, the International Relations Committee of the American Library Association has developed 'Criteria for the Selection of Consultants to Serve Abroad' (see Appendix 1). Included in that list is the mandate that the Association develop a roster of qualified consultants. Other national associations could develop similar lists within their countries and the cumulation of these lists could be combined into an international data base maintained by IFLA. Annually updated, this data base could provide a first step in creating an appropriate resource for consultants search. Thus a broader base would be established for international organizations and countries to search for better matches between job descriptions and consultants qualifications. The problem is to contact a variety of appropriate skills, not simply those in favor with national organizations, and to provide a mechanism for evaluation of consultants. In addition, such a clearinghouse managed with IFLA might encourage a 'two-way' flow of consultants, including use of experts from so-called 'developing countries' and already developed countries. We have much to learn from each other.

The Consulting Process: Things to Ask or Know before a Project Begins

Depending upon the level of complexity of a given project, anywhere from a single consultant to several teams and hundreds of individual activities may be involved. To be sure, this latter type is rare; but consider the vast social project for libraries in Iran in the early 1970s with Nasser Sharify. In order to assure that both consultant and employer are in agreement as to the process, development and anticipated outcomes, a structured process is desirable. The key phases in the planning and development of such a project might be organized along the line of a traditional management model:

 1. Acquire environmental knowledge, political/cultural/professional, etc.
 2. Establishment of understanding of the perceived problem.
 3. Diagnose actual problem.
 4. Feedback to client.
 5. Establish understanding.
 6. Preliminary goal and position statement.
 7. Commitment to the project.
 8. Resource analysis.
 9. Conceptual planning.
10. Plan approval.
11. Master planning.
12. Final commitment.
13. Staged implementation.
14. Evaluation and redirection of plan.

In reality, however, the consulting process is seldom so organized and may involve constant re-evaluation and redefinition of the project's parameters. Answers to certain basic questions by the library agency should be provided for the consultant including the following:

1. What is the nature of the problem to be addressed?
2. What are the anticipated outcomes of employing a consultant?
3. With whom will the consultant or consultants work?
4. What is the history of the problem and what alternatives have been proposed and rejected or accepted and failed?
5. What are the parameters of the problem, time constraints, budget requirements and staff allocations?
6. What previous studies relate to this topic?

While it is important to establish understanding as a first step in the consulting process, invariably there are differences between paper descriptions of employment conditions, expectations and environment and the reality of the situation. It is often essential to go through the process of establishing a contract with the client, if a suitable and workable report is to be prepared.

Consultants are involved in a variety of levels of activity, ranging from high level policy intervention (in which the consultant is asked to represent the library or the agency and act as an advocate for a particular program, project or policy) to specifically defined and contained projects within the library or agency itself. Other levels of activity may be inter-organizations in nature, requiring the consultant to act as a mediator in the development of, for example, resource sharing, library systems, or networks. Still other projects may be more specific, such as the development of a serials data base, a special collection or training project.

The consultant's grasp of the national reality of the situation is often limited. In a small town in the Colombian mountains Unesco sent a doctor to help establish a regional clinic. Upon arrival the doctor, to his dismay found that surgical instruments were being sterilized by boiling. He was quite disturbed at the lack of suitable equipment and immediately requested an autoclave. The most expensive autoclave arrived in due time and the doctor proudly plugged it in and prepared for an operation, assuming that he could use his new gadget to sterilize the instruments. No sooner had the autoclave been plugged in than not only did the lights in the hospital go out but the generator for the whole town was blown out and did not operate again for a week. The autoclave, to my knowledge, still sits in the rural hospital, a monument to modern technology and its uselessness in certain situations. So, too, the library consultant must be careful to propose appropriate solutions, not simply cosmetic changes from his or her own country. Alternatives should be appropriate to the environment in which they will exist. There is an example of a country striving to develop a library school and national library. Staff is comprised mainly of in-house trained librarians with a few masters level librarians who have trained abroad. Not surprisingly, an extra-national expert was brought in to help in the planning for these agencies.

Among that consultant's recommendations was one better suited to developed countries, namely that the library employ only masters level librarians. No interim process or training program was indicated. How unrealistic, yet not atypical of unimplemented plans proposed by inflexible consultants whose perceptions of local realities are clearly based on home environment.

The consultant often becomes a 'point of reference' for the development of a particular. Even when the report is tendered or the project officially completed, for the consultant, the rippling effects of even a short term of consultancy may be far reaching. For example, there is the question of professional commitment, and of the invisible college, of professional and personal contact that continue far beyond the limitation of a consulting contact. This may involve advice on future plans, on additional consultants, on the training of personnel in library schools abroad.

It is important to realize that both the employer and the consultant assume a risk in the contractual process. While employers are wagering budget allocations and scarce resources, they retain the prerogative to replace a consultant or reject a final report and seek additional advice. Consultants, on the other hand, risk their reputations with each project and their future job prospects. Reputations will either be enhanced or diminished as a function of the satisfaction of the employer. In cases where the host library or site for the project differs from the actual employer (such as an international agency) the possibility of satisfying both agencies may be difficult. The international agency may have outlined one plan or action or approach and the host country may have its own agenda. To whom is the consultant responsible? If the host library is not satisfied then the consultant has not fulfilled his mission; on the other hand, if the international agency is not pleased then the consultant is not likely to secure employment from that source in the near future. Consultants should be careful to choose projects for which they possess the necessary skills or can amass a team with such skills. In other words a project in which there is a good chance of success and in which the requirements of the job are clearly delineated. A brief summary of the consultant-employer situation may be stated as 'Let the employer beware, the consultant take care'.

In response to the broad general outline of the consulting process, emphasizing the need for intercultural communication and adaptation the national reality of the reactors drawing on a variety of personal experiences from all areas of the world brought additional problems and questions to the attention of the forum.

The following list of important facts to be considered in the consulting process is a synthesis of the comments made by the reactors during IFLA's Standing Committee on Theory and Research's panel discussion in Manila. In reviewing the transcript of the session, it is interesting to note the common themes which emerged in the comments of the reactors from the developing countries who have received a number of invited as well as 'surprise' consultants, and the consultants themselves who have worked in developing countries.

Important Factors

1. The consultant must have or be able to achieve a thorough knowledge of the environment, politically and culturally as well as an understanding of the role of the library and its administrative constraints.
2. Clear definition of the problems and a realistic expectation as to the goals and objectives of the project before the consultant is chosen.
3. An understanding of the cultural, academic and experiential background of the consultant as major factors in their selection.
4. A development approach to the selection of consultants, which involves the local staff.
5. More reliance on local experts and experts from the same regions.
6. Consensual agreement between the local staff and the consultant as to the

problem, goals and objectives of the project and a realistic agreement about the anticipated results of the consultant's work.
7. Involvement of local staff at all levels of activities, with particular emphasis on project continuation beyond the limits of the consultant's tenure.
8. Emphasis on bi-directional flow of communication between consultants and local staff.
9. Clearly determined parameters for the consultants, especially those with access to the administerial levels.
10. Feedback from consultants and local staff to international agencies.
11. Promotion of exchange of information among developing countries.
12. Outside evaluation of projects whenever possible.

Appendix I

American Library Association, International Relations Committee
Criteria for the Selection of Consultants to Serve Abroad

The American Library Association (ALA), serving the public interest, assigns a high priority to the development of libraries, librarianship, and information services throughout the world. ALA reaffirms its continuing desire to foster international library development in all countries, and in return hopes to continue to learn from its participation.

In response to requests for assistance from abroad, ALA must be able to recommend librarians and information specialists who are both highly qualified and sensitive to cultural and national differences. Such consultants must be able to respond to well-qualified foreign colleagues who are prepared to consider, within their own national and professional context and resources, any advice or suggestions made by consultants.

International library consultants need to be alert to the ambivalence with which recommendations and advice may be received at any time; therefore, when offering their considered opinions, they must be especially sensitive to the professional accomplishments and national pride of their foreign hosts.

ALA will apply the following guidelines and criteria in recommending, nominating, and selecting international consultants.

General professional objectives

1. Learn in depth the situation of the host country in its political, social, and professional aspects.
2. Make certain the problem is correctly understood and established.
3. Establish contacts with educated persons in the host country who feel themselves to have valuable perceptions and ideas which they want to see reflected in the consultant's proposals.
4. Encourage, when appropriate, the establishment of internships or short

term assignments for nationals of host countries; however, this concept must be used carefully so as not to exaggerate expectations of the interns.
5. Initiate local planning conferences with experts from local institutions.
6. Present a report which clearly defines the problems and presents solutions which are sensitive to the culture of the country and relate to its library needs.

Consultants should possess the following:

Professional qualifications
1. Broad library background with appropriate specializations.
2. Conversant with current library theories and practice.
3. Broad knowledge of library and library related organizations, information services and networks.
4. Broad professional contacts.
5. Practical management or operational experience.
6. Conceptual orientation.
7. Experience in standard setting and implementation.

Personal qualifications
1. Appreciative of attitudes and views of person from other countries and different cultural or ethnic backgrounds.
2. Receptive to new ideas.
3. Skilled in interpersonal relations.
4. Knowledgeable or skilled in a foreign language; if possible in the language of the host country.
5. Knowledgeable in social, political, and cultural affairs.
6. Experience in working abroad.
7. Skilled in listening and in oral and written expression.

The Association's responsibility
1. It is recognized that consultantships can sharpen and broaden professional qualifications and give consultants a valuable understanding of program quality, operational techniques, and managerial competence. Therefore it is the responsibility of ALA to encourage consultancies of highest professional standards.
2. The Association should make clear to foreign governments and institutions that when recommending consultants it follows its stated policy which does not condone violations to human rights or discrimination by race, color, sex, religion, or national origin.
3. The Association should announce in *American Libraries* and other appropriate publications or circulars, requests for library consultants which are received from organizations and institutions here or abroad; it should also publicize the international activities and work of professionals so engaged.
4. The Association through its International Relations Committee (IRC) and International Relations Officer (IRO) should provide coordination of consultants' activities and establish a working list of qualified consultants.
5. The Association requests copies of reports be filed with IRO. ALA members

who act as consultants under other agencies are requested to file copies of their reports with IRO.

Notes

This article was first published in *International Library Review*, Volume 14, pages 379-90, 1982, and is reprinted here with the kind permission of the authors and Academic Press Inc. (London) Limited.

1. James Lockwood (1977). 'Involving consultants in library change, *College and Research Libraries* **33**, 498-503.
2. Edward C. Stewart (n.d.) 'The survival stage of intercultural communications' (photocopy). For more information on Stewart's theories of intercultural and cross-cultural communications, *see*, Edward C. Stewart (1972), *American Cultural Patterns: Cross Cultural Perspective*, LaGrange Park, Ill., Intercultural Network.
3. *ibid.*
4. Lockwood, p. 502.

On the Librarianship of Poverty

K. J. Mchombu

This paper attempts to outline the main characteristics of librarianship under the conditions of *poverty*. To the best of my knowledge and conviction, this is the base on which any meaningful discussion of information work in underdeveloped countries should be firmly anchored.

The goal of my paper is to set up and elaborate on four principles that, in my view, determine the social relevance of information work in developing countries. This is a personal testament, and I hasten to add that the views expressed hereafter do not necessarily represent the offical position of my employers—the Tanzania Library Service. Similarly, criticism is not directed at any particular institution or person. Should it appear so, I offer my sincere apologies.

Relevance to Society

If their work is to be relevant to society, information workers must formulate terms of reference that are consistent with the needs of underdeveloped societies. At the moment, it seems to me that such terms of reference are largely non-existent, and where they do exist they are vague and frequently irrelevant. Below are the principles, which are not mutually exclusive, that I believe can help in formulating the appropriate terms of reference (and justify the sweeping statements above):

1. That the chief factor determining information work in developing countries should be poverty rather than affluence.
2. That information work in developing countries differs markedly from information work in developed countries.
3. That it is possible to gather a body of knowledge on how best to meet this challenge.

© 1982 Munksgaard, Copenhagen

4. That information workers must play an active role in the process of socio-economic development.

Information Work and Poverty

In stating that information work in underdeveloped countries should be based on poverty, I am saying something that could well be embarrassingly self-evident. The division of the world into a rich North and a poor South is not only reflected in different levels of income, and the sharp difference in most things that make life bearable, but it divides the provision of information with equal clarity.

In underdeveloped countries the common man is poor, illiterate and concerned with the basics of survival; more than four-fifths of his income is spent on food alone. He is hungry, undernourished, and diseases such as malaria, sleeping sickness and cholera are his constant companions. Children suffer more than adults; kwashiakor and parasitic diseases claim many of their lives before they reach the age of ten. Only about 40 per cent of the children complete primary school.

More than 90 per cent of the people live in rural areas where transport and communication are very difficult. Within the urban areas, outside the enclaves inhabited by the elite, the majority of people live in slums, the so-called, 'Shanty towns'. The dwellings are overcrowded, and the level of housing is hopeless by any standards, human or otherwise.

Under-employment and unemployment is widespread, and it is not national income that grows steadily year by year, but human deprivation and suffering. Another growth area concerns the birth rate, at 3 per cent per year it is the 'best' in the world.

This anatomy of poverty and social reality must surely determine the nature, objectives and philosophy of librarianship in underdeveloped countries. Poverty dictates, for example, the pattern of information services where the amount of money available per head is less than 1 shilling (10 pence). Such poverty is responsible for a lack of trained staff, a weak publishing industry, and half-empty shelves—in short, this is a distinct and different world, one ruled by poverty, ignorance and disease. The factors outlined above are a formidable challenge to the *information worker* in underdeveloped countries and give information work a very different quality.

At this point there are three questions that need to be asked. What fundamental knowledge and skills does an information worker need to work efficiently in such a situation? How can this knowledge be applied to the maximum benefit of the underdeveloped society? Is it possible to gather a body of knowledge on how best to meet this challenge? I cannot pretend to have ready-made answers. Obviously, a considerable amount of interdisciplinary research to these questions is needed to provide the answers required. However, a number of observations can be made.

Conferences and journals create, in my view, the right environment in which strategies can be developed for best meeting these problems and assembling the required knowledge and skills of optimum use to information workers in developing countries.

A Body of Knowledge to Meet Such Challenges

My firm belief that it is quite possible to gather together a body of knowledge on how this challenge is best met was stated implicitly above. Such a task requires, primarily, a particular attitude of mind, and secondarily, a suitable methodology that will give the desired results.

The attitude required is one of open-mindedness and objectivity. We must be prepared to subject every aspect of librarianship to vigorous criticism and evaluation because, like it or not, we have to start from the known before moving on to the unknown. Through this selective adaption, it is possible to produce a considerable body of knowledge suitable for the needs of underdeveloped countries. The rest of the knowledge needed will, however, have to be derived from the existing situation and unique problems.

This will be a classic case of theories evolving from practice, rather than of theories being borrowed from abroad and applied misguidedly in a very different context. I dare to suggest that it is possible to produce a distinct body of knowledge suited to the needs of underdeveloped countries using these two methods.

At first, such knowledge will lack form; clearly defined limits and the harmony between one area and another may not always be apparent. Its strong potential will, however, lie in the fact that it is theoretical knowledge that has developed out of existing social problems. It will not be knowledge imported wholesale that is abstract and frequently irrelevant. Such knowledge could well be closer to sociology and the economics of underdevelopment than to traditional librarianship, as understood and practised in the majority of underdeveloped countries today.

The critical part of this exercise is establishing what is relevant to a particular situation at a particular moment. It is this situational relevance that will shape the new theory of the librarianship of poverty. Using this approach it could be possible to develop a theoretical framework regarding the following fields:

1. The pattern of information services.
2. The role of information workers.
3. Existing social factors and their implications for information workers.
4. Relationship between information work and socio-economic development.

Before proceeding to explore these four fields, I feel it should be emphasized that our colleagues, the economists, sociologists, political scientists and educators, have done much work aimed at developing a theoretical base for their professions that is relevant to underdeveloped countries. With careful interdisciplinary comparative studies, we could learn a lot that would be of great value in this undertaking—if only we could for a moment think beyond our hallowed DDC's, Sears Lists, and cataloguing rules.

Information Services Must Reflect the Resources of the Country

This statement may be thought to be self-evident if it is realized that information infrastructure depends on an economic base for financial support. In practice, however, most 'planners' of information units are not free of pre-conceived notions imported from the developed countries in which they did their training. The standards suggested for libraries in underdeveloped areas are often faithfully copied from British, American or Australian handbooks.

I suggest that an objective atttitude may force it upon us that a fresh set of standards more closely related to the actual situation is needed. A start must be made from the basic position that the limited resources must be stretched to provide maximum social benefit. However, social benefit is a concept not easy to measure. It is easy to confuse means with ends. Very often we take pride in giving 'statistics' covering library buildings constructed within the past five years, the number of motor vehicles purchased, and the librarians and technicians sent for training. This emphasis is sadly misplaced. It is like a motor-car manufacturer who tries to maximize not his output of cars but the number of his workers and the size of his factory.

Given a sum of money, say four million shillings (£200,000), we should be able to find out which alternative programme of expenditure would be of greatest benefit. Using cost beneift, and cost-effectiveness methods, we could establish the cheapest path to our goal. We could focus on the end product rather than the means.

These conditions of poverty mean that the need to make the most of limited resources in the provision of information services is a basic strategy. The construction of libraries, the training of librarians and the purchase of motor vehicles are merely means to an end—they are not the goal of an information unit in itself. The key question is, how many more people can we serve as a result of a certain item of expenditure?

Considering the majority of information units, we find that the wage bill is around 60 per cent and the capital costs are very high. These two items of expenditure have hampered considerably the development of information services in most underdeveloped countries. The ridiculous situation where there are cataloguers who are without incoming documents is all too common.

High capital expenditure is the outcome of trying to construct premises modelled on those existing in Europe and North America. The buildings are splendid, but because resources are severely limited, it means that only one or two of these imposing monuments can be erected in a decade. The process of spreading an information infrastructure throughout a country is considerably delayed by the adoption of this expensive policy. If we use cost benefit methods, we may yet discover that it is the cheap, small, well-maintained buildings made of inexpensive building materials that are an important key to the faster growth of our information services.

All this leads to the conclusion that the standards of information services must be tailored to the economic ability of a country. If the pattern of information services is pushed ahead of general economic development, standards will be set that can only be maintained in small pockets of the country. The lucky few may have a very good service, but most people will have no service at all, or a service that is inadequate and at prohibitive distances.

The planning of information services in developing countries needs to be deliberately related to a particular time and place. The temptation to upgrade standards, complexity, and sophistication before extending coverage needs to be checked, for this 'keeping up with the Joneses' results in prestige programmes that do little to extend the coverage of information services while absorbing large sums of money and pools of skill.

There is yet another reason why plans having a low capital output ratio are to be preferred. Most developing countries have a constantly fluctuating economy because this depends on the export of a few main crops or products—so that as world prices fluctuate the economy alternates from slump to boom and back again in bewildering succession. Government revenues that depend on such earnings reflect these cycles—expensive plans initiated during boom periods act as a painful drain on funds during periods of slump.

The Role of Information Workers

Most of the staff holding senior positions in underdeveloped countries have been trained in information work as practised in industrialized countries. Not unexpectedly, the prevailing attitude is that this is the way in which users should behave, and the way in which information services operate. My belief, already stated, is that this is an erroneous view of things because the lavish standards of service that exist in a typical developed country are impossible to maintain in a poor country, unless the objective is to provide an information service for the fortunate few rather than the majority of mankind in developing societies. Indeed, this does, sadly, appear to be the unstated objective of many an information service in developing countries. After more than fifteen years of existence, and expenditure of millions of shillings, many public library systems have not yet succeeded in serving more than 1 per cent of the population of their areas.

In most underdeveloped countries, the number of documents per head is low, the average sum spent annually per head of the population is low, and trained staff per head of population is low. Despite these facts, a few favoured areas enjoy a standard of service shaped to European standards. If it took fifteen years to reach 1 per cent of the population, how long will it take to reach the remaining 99 per cent? Will it take 99 × 15 years to serve the whole population? If the present trend continues, I am afraid this could be the case. We could unwittingly provide a service such as that characterized by Bill (1962):

> a service supposedly for all, used by only a smallish minority, and found wanting by most.

In the area of manpower planning, care must be taken that the staff required are produced in sufficient quantities to keep pace with the development of the service. Because of the scarcity of resources, greater emphasis may have to be placed on technicians rather than on librarians.

In underdeveloped countries technicians play a different and more important role because of the shortage of librarians, and this situation will continue for the coming decade. The work done by technicians includes tasks such as cataloguing, indexing, readers' advisory work, bibliographic and literature searches—this is work of a more skilled nature than that done by their counterparts in developed countries—because there is no one else to do it.

The shortage of staff can be alleviated if all trained staff are made aware of their obligation to train those working under them. This approach will ensure a snowball effect, because the trained staff will themselves carry out training activities in their own information units.

The scarcity of everything would seem to indicate that co-operation between information units should result in economizing on resources and overall benefits. Yet, as found in most underdeveloped countries, it is one thing to agree on the importance of co-operation, but a very different thing to practise it. There are some psychological barriers to co-operation that need to be overcome if libraries are to co-operate in our countries.

As already pointed out above, underdeveloped countries have very limited job and career opportunities. Attempts at initiating co-operative ventures are regarded with suspicion because the individuals concerned regard each other as potential rivals. Those with similar qualifications, working in the same field, regard anything achieved by someone else as a threat to their own position in this imaginary but fierce struggle for survival. It is rare indeed to come across anyone prepared to subordinate his own interests to some broader social goal.

Furthermore, an exchange of fruitful ideas is something difficult because a senior person will not risk a loss of face by being seen to act on the advice or recommendation of anyone else—especially a junior—since this would seem to indicate that he acknowledges the superiority of someone else.

The conspicuous absence of union catalogues, union lists of serials and centralized cataloguing schemes, more than testifies to this psychological problem. Unless information workers come to realize that it is only by working as a group rather than against one another, that they can achieve their objectives and demonstrate to society what they are capable of doing—continued isolation and 'one-up-manship' is a source of weakness and leads to overall ineffectiveness.

Existing Social Factors and their Implications for Information Workers

A number of existing social factors, lack of resources, plans based on Washington and London standards, and psychological insecurity of information workers making co-operation impossible, etc., were considered in the previous sections of this paper. A further area not yet explored is education and the contradictory attitude of society towards this subject.

It has been pointed out by many a good writer that education is the main correlate of reading and library use, hence the greater the level of education, the greater the likelihood for utilizing library services. However, seen in the light of the experience of underdeveloped countries, this generalization is not always true.

The decisive factor, is not just 'education' alone; the kind of education that a person receives also determines the likelihood of his continued use of libraries and information services in the community. To a very large extent, formal education in underdeveloped societies is dominated by cultural attitudes towards authority—be it parental, religious or political. The readily accepted attitude is to obey these sources of authority without question. The classroom is a microcosm of the larger society outside; education is largely an unquestioning acceptance of the teaching authority. Books and any reading matter play only a minor part in the process. Lecture notes and a single textbook can see a student through his academic career. There is little opportunity for innovation, experimentation, and objective analysis—even at university level.

It is quite plain that every aspect of our education system tends to discourage the formation of wide reading habits. Out of class, reading tasks are seldom assigned, or assigned as a mere formality. Should a student be bold enough to read widely and formulate his own ideas, or ideas in conflict with his class lectures, then he may well fail his examinations.

This narrow-mindedness is considerably reinforced by the examination system in most underdeveloped countries. Because of the limited opportunities available in secondary and higher education, the purpose of examinations has now become not a test of a student's mastery of his subject, but primarily an obstacle to reduce drastically the number of those who go on to higher studies.

Having surmounted this hurdle, through fair means or foul, this tiny group assume the mental attitude of an elite—that they possess particular natural qualifications that are lacking in others. This pseudo-intellectual arrogance has often been articulated by the statement; 'After graduation, the only thing I will ever read is the sports page of the daily newspapers'.

This specific educational context has resulted in library services in underdeveloped countries having very limited demands—most of the stock is left permanently idle on the shelves to collect dust. The social pressure to expand library services is minimal—to the majority libraries have little social relevance. Not unexpectedly, the role of library services is still a limited one, and the status of this profession comparatively low.

Many librarians and government officials have failed to discern these underlying factors. Attempts to solve the problems have included the hiring of experts to advise on how to start information units and systems; the formulation of standards copied from Western countries, or requested for foreign aid. To date, most such efforts have not lived up to expectations. The foreign nationals leave the country and their model libraries speedily deteriorate to their former shambles, their text-book reports being filed away out of sight. The standards formulated fail to elicit any action other than temporary curiosity. Foreign aid continues to pour dollars, pounds, kroner and Deutschemarks into the country. The slight impact that this aid has had proves that it is only of secondary importance in the development of information services; money alone does not create an information system that involves readers, premises, documents and staff. What is of primary importance for such services is local desire and initiative. Foreign aid can help but will never be decisive in the development of information services in underdeveloped countries. In fact, its periodic availability may deceive planners into indulging in expensive plans left half finished when such aid comes to an end; or acquiring expensive gadgets for which no spare parts or software are forthcoming when the donors leave.

Relationship Between Information Work and Socio-economic Development

Socio-economic development concerns every organisation in underdeveloped societies. Information units cannot continue to isolate themselves from this social struggle aimed at giving people a better life. Every worker in an information unit must study this historical process so as to determine what is expected of him. Anyone who shirks this task risks redundancy because, in the distribution of scarce resources, only those who can demonstrate that they are capable of producing a favourable cost benefit balance will deserve the funds required. We have no right to expect anything else.

I suggest that having the right attitude is the most important factor in determining how actively information services will be involved in this struggle for survival. There is a need to be seen to provide information geared to development in the fields of agriculture, industry, commerce, education and health. Unfortunately, the majority of information workers in underdeveloped societies are timid in their approach and have a limited vision of activities and ways in which information services can participate in this social struggle. I strongly believe that an information worker devoted to national development, having a sense of mission and commitment to this social struggle, and understanding the importance and urgency of modernization is likely to play an active and fully involved role. It is perhaps quite plain, too, that an information worker conditioned to view his job from European standards may come to consider his environment as backward and hopeless, and become a disillusioned misfit. On the other hand, an information worker who treats his environment as a positive challenge to be met and finally altered for the better, can become an involved agent of change.

It is only through such involvement in the struggle against the social enemies of poverty, ignorance and disease that the relevance of information services can be firmly established. It takes hard thinking, hard work and patience.

Summary

This paper attempts to examine how information services can be developed under conditions of poverty. Information workers must formulate terms of reference for their work consistent with the needs of underdeveloped countries. As this work has to be carried out under conditions of extreme poverty, scant resources must be streched to provide maximum benefit. Means must not be confused with ends: buildings, motor vehicles and wages are not the objective, hence expenditure on these items can only be justified if it results in an increased number of users.

In order to develop a body of knowledge on how best to meet these challenges, an open-minded and objective attitude is needed. The methods that can be used to gather this body of knowledge include adaptation and experimentation relating to practical problems. The scarcity of resources must be reflected by the pattern of information services, the role of information workers, the way that information services are adapted to the locality concerned and the active participation of information workers in national development.

The pattern of information services must reflect the economic ability of the country concerned rather than follow standards copied blindly from developed countries. The cost benefit concept is vital in ensuring the optimum use of scant resources and that the cheapest alternative is followed. The pattern of information services needs to be approached from the bottom upwards rather than from the top downwards. Small, cheap units, located close to where people actually live, must come before large, sophisticated libraries.

Information workers need to develop an aggressive attitude and to participate fully in the social struggle for national development. There is also a need for co-opertion in order to economize on scant resources. To achieve this, the present psychological problems must be rationalized and overcome. These are the result of the limited career opportunities available that lead people to regard others as rivals, and consider the accomplishments of others as a threat to their own positions. Another problem is a retrogressive educational system that depends wholly on the teaching authority, and on a single text-book. Such a system does not lead to the formation of wide reading habits.

The conclusion is that information workers must look for solutions to their problems within their own societies rather than depending on foreign aid.

References

This article was first published in *Libri*, **33**, 3, pp. 241–50, 1982, and reprinted here with the kind permission of Munksgaard International Publishers Limited.

1. Asheim, L. *Librarianship in the Developing Countries*. Urbana, Illiniois, 1966.
2. Bill, A. H. 'The Library in the Community', in *Proceedings of the Annual Conference*. The Library Association, 1962, p. 63.
3. Ilomo, C. S. 'Paraprofessional Library Training in Tanzania'. (mimeograph).
4. Mchombu, K. J. 'Information studies programme for Tanzania: a proposal', Loughborough, 1979. (unpublished M.A. thesis).
5. Minder, T. and B. Whitten. 'Basic Undergraduate Education for Librarianship and Information Science', *Journal of Education for Librarianship*, **15**, 4, 1974, pp. 258–70.
6. Kotei, S. I-A. 'Preparing Teaching Materials for Library Education in Ghana: a Historical Account.' Critics meeting, Arusha, 25–30 November 1979.

The Bibliography

1. Abdo, Mekhag S.
   University of Qatar new buildings—(mission) 30 July 1982. 7p.
   Keywords: educational buildings; universities; Qatar—library buildings; university libraries.
   UNESCO DOC. CODE: FMR/900/QAT/13/End of assignment report. MICROFICHE: 83fr0038. (Restricted).

2. Abid, Abdelaziz; Bonnichon, Monique.
   Évaluation du project de démarrage du Réseau sahélien d'information et de documentation scientifiques et techniques: Comité permanent inter-États de lutte contre la sécheresse au Sahel—(mission) 17 March 1983. 32p., illus.
   Keywords: scientific information systems; information/library networks; information systems evaluation; Sahel; French speaking Africa; Central Africa—information processing; minicomputers; documentation centres; computer software; referral centres, information user needs; information/library cooperation; project design; project implementation; project evaluation. **Identifiers:** Comité permanent inter-États de lutte contre la sécheresse au Sahel. Réseau sahélien d'information et de documentation scientifiques et techniques.
   UNESCO DOC. CODE: FMR/PGI/83/111; RP/1981-83/5/10.1/03/ Rapport technique. MICROFICHE: 83fr0123. (Restricted).

3. Abul Hasan.
   Reorganization of the National Book Centre: Bangladesh—(mission) 31 December 1980. 7p., in various pagings.

Keywords: book development; book production; book distribution; publishing; Bangladesh. **Identifiers:** National Book Centre (Bangladesh).

UNESCO DOC. CODE: FMR/CC/BCE/80/198; RP/1979–80/4/3/5/07/Assignment report. MICROFICHE: 81fr0074. (Restricted).

4. Acland, A.W.
The establishment of a film and video production unit: film-video and photographic archive and resources centre: Regional—(mission) 10–18 December 1976. January 1977. 27p.

Mission report on the establishment of a film-making unit, a video recording unit, and an audiovisual resource centre at the headquarters of the League of Arab States in Egypt—describes the present scope of the information service for the dissemination of information; provides proposals for film-making and the establishment of regional audiovisual archives, including videotape recordings; mentions archive facilities, archive records preservation and film-making training.

Keywords: film-making; video recordings; multimedia resource centres; Arab States; Egypt—information services; dissemination of information; audiovisual archives; videotape recording; archive facilities; archive records preservation; film-making training. **Identifiers:** League of Arab States.

UNESCO DOC. CODE: FMR/CC/DCS/77/101; RP/1975–76/4.131.3/End-of-assignment report. MICROFICHE: 78fr0144.

5. Adams, Scott; Madkour, Mohamed A.; Slamecka, Valadimir.
Proposed national information policy of Egypt. Atlanta, GA.: Georgia Institute of Technology, School of Information and Computer Science, September 1981. vi, 29p.

Keywords: science and technology; information services; government policies; Egypt—national planning; problem solving; manpower utilization; data transmission; communications management; institution building; libraries.

U.S. NATIONAL SCIENCE FOUNDATION CONTRACT NO. INT-7924187; PASA NF/EGY-0016-7-77. DOC. NO. PN-AAP-152.

6. Adamson, Colin; Vasudevan, Mullath; Vorwerk, Claus.
Development of the Yarmouk University: Hashemite Kingdom of Jordan—(mission) 20 August 1977. 75p.

Mission report on educational development in the field of higher education at a new university of Jordan, dealing specifically with educational management, manpower needs and the establishment of a university information system—discusses the educational administrative structure and the structure of the university currriculum which lays emphasis on science education and higher technical education; includes enrolment projections and projected requirements for academic teaching personnel and educational administrators; devotes a section to the development of information services with special emphasis on information processing.

Keywords: education development; higher education; universities; Jordan; educational management; manpower needs; information systems—educational administrative structure; university curriculum; science education; higher technical education; enrolment projections; academic teaching personnel; educational administrators; information services; information processing. **Identifiers:** Yarmouk University (Jordan).

UNESCO DOC. CODE: FMR/ED/HEP/77/185; RP/1977–78/1.171.6/Technical report. MICROFICHE: 78fr0055. (Restricted).

7. Akaboshi, Takako.
Les Bibliothèques scolaires au Maroc—(mission) 12 October 1979. 28p., incl. bibl.

Keywords: school libraries; information/library development; Morocco—primary education; secondary education; information/library administration; information/library facilities; information/library personnel; information/library budgets; library collections.

UNESCO DOC. CODE: FMR/PGI/79/245 (UNDP); UNDP/MOR/74/003/Rapport de mission. MICROFICHE: 80fr0010. (Restricted).

8. Akita, J.M.
Development of the National Archives and the National Documentation centre: Uganda—(mission) 1979. 49p., illus.

Keywords: national archives; archive development; documentation centre; Uganda—archive legislation; archive records preservation; archive personnel; archive science training, archive facilities; administrative structure. **Identifiers:**

National Archives (Uganda). National Documentation Centre (Uganda).
UNESCO DOC. CODE: FMR/BEP/PGI/79/105; PP/1977–78/5.1.5/Technical report. MICROFICHE: 79fr0189. (Restricted).

9. Ali, Romdhane.
Organisation des services d'information pour ALDOC: Ligue des États Arabes—(mission) 31 December 1980. 22p., illus.

Keywords: information services; scientific information systems; information user needs; information/library planning; Arab States—information/library financing; information sources; information/library personnel; computer hardware; information/library facilities; information processing automation. **Identifiers:** Centre for Documentation and Information of the Arab League.
UNESCO DOC. CODE: FMR/PGI/OPS/80/259 (UNDP); UNDP/RAB/79/030/Rapport de mission. MICROFICHE: 81fr0093. (Restricted).

10. Aman, Mohammed M.
ALDOC staff training programme: League of Arab States, Tunis—(mission) 31 December 1981. 12p., incl. bibl.

Keywords: information science training; training methods; training courses; information/library personnel; documentation centres; Arab States—in-service training; training abroad; curriculum development. **Identifiers:** League of Arab States, Documentation Centre.
UNESCO DOC. CODE: FMR/PGI/OPS/81/403 (UNDP); UNDP/RAB/79/030/Assignment report. MICROFICHE: 82fr0009. (Restricted).

11. Aman, Mohammad M.
Broad system outline for ALDOC: League of Arab States—(mission) 31 December 1980. 67p., illus., plans.

Keywords: scientific information systems; information services; information/library planning; systems analysis; Arab States—information user needs; data processing; information science training; information/library personnel; job description; information processing automation; information/library facilities; information/library budgets; information/library administration; information/library opertions; curriculum development; computer hardware. **Identifiers:** Centre for Documentation and Information of the Arab League.

UNESCO DOC. CODE: FMR/PGI/OPS/80/257 (UNDP); UNDP/RAB/79/030/Assignment report. MICROFICHE: 81fr0095. (Restricted).

12. Aman, Mohammed M.
Documentation and library services of the Ministry of Information: Hashemite Kingdom of Jordan—(mission) 31 December 1980. 35p.

Keywords: information services; scientific information systems; information/library planning; Jordan—socio-economic factors; educational systems; mass media; information/library administration; administrative structure; information/library policy; broadcasting; information/library personnel; information science training; information materials; library equipment; information processing. **Identifiers:** Jordan, Ministry of Information, Directorate of Press and Publications.

UNESCO DOC. CODE: FMR/PGI/80/193; RP/1979–80/5/10/1/05/ Technical report. MICROFICHE: 81fr0062. (Restricted).

13. Aman, Mohammed M.
Plan for a documentation centre for the Ministry of Education: State of Bahrain—(mission) 14 November–1 December 1976. 15 February 1977. 12p., incl. bibl.

Mission report on the development of a documentation centre for educational documentation at the Ministry of Education in Bahrain—outlines the administrative structure of the existing documentation unit noting the lack of qualified documentation/library personnel; recommends the strengthening of the library collection for educational research and the expansion of bibliographic services at present being provided.

Keywords: documentation centre; educational information; Ministry; Bahrain—administrative structure; information/library personnel; library collections; educational research; bibliographic services. **Identifiers:** Bahrain, Ministry of Education.

UNESCO DOC. CODE: FMR/PGI/77/122; PP/1975–76/4.221.4/ Technical report. MICROFICHE: 78fr0034. (Restricted).

14. Antonelli, G.
Mise sur pied d'un service national d'archives et de pré-archivage: Liban—(mission) mai-juin 1974. October 1974. 57p.

Mission report dealing with archive planning in Lebanon—describes a project for reorganizing the national archives and discusses the relevant documentation/library legislation; gives recommendations for archive administration and records management.

UNESCO DOC. CODE: 3087/RMO.RD/DBA. MICROFICHE: 75fr0015. (Restricted).

15. Anwar, Mumtaz A.; Khan, Bashir Ali; Schabel, Donald; Tiwana, Nazar.
Integrated Rural Information System: a preliminary report on the organization of libraries and information networks in Pakistan. March 1976.

A study of the various schemes being implemented by the government of Pakistan (Integrated Rural Development, Health and Population Planning, Adult Education, People's Open University, People-Oriented Public Libraries, etc.) has led to the development of a new approach in order to help achieve the development objectives of these programmes. The scheme is proposed in a report prepared by a team of United States and Pakistan librarians. It is essentially an extension of the People-Oriented Public Libraries programme and envisages bringing the adult education, educational television and People's Open University programmes into the people's library. It also visualizes the people's library to play a supportive role by providing means for updating information and continuing education.

The idea of combining several services into one unit and providing supportive services to other development projects has taken the form of the new concept of Integrated Rural Information System (IRIS). The IRIS visualizes the development of an information centre (people's library) for a population of reasonable size to serve as the receiving end of all information inputs of various development programmes and disseminating point of the information inputs received at the community level.

This unit will be the bottom tier of the National Information System (NATIS) which, when fully developed, will consist of people's provincial libraries, people's district libraries, people's tehsil libraries, and people's libraries at the local level (both urban and rural). The national library will be at the top of the system and will also serve as a co-ordinating agency.

ERIC: ED 125620/IR 003708.

16. Arnaud, Paul.
Establishment of an information system at Yarmouk University: Hashemite Kingdom of Jordan—(mission) 1 December 1980. 28p. (in various pagings), illus., incl. bibl.

Keywords: management information systems; information services; universities; Jordan—information network; information sources; information user needs; systems analysis; decision making; university libraries; information/library management; questionnaires. **Identifiers:** Yarmouk University (Jordan).

UNESCO DOC. CODE: FMR/PGI/OPS/80/247 (SP); JORDAN/ Assignment report. MICROFICHE: 81fr0005. (Restricted).

17. Arnold, G.W.
University of Wyoming Afghanistan contract with the Agency for International Development—final report 1973. Laramie, WY.: University of Wyoming, 30 June 1973.

Keywords: Afghanistan; Reference library.

U.S.A.I.D. CONTRACT NO. AID/NESA-215. DOC. NO. B 306009200 6801 Final Report. (MICROFICHE: not available).

18. Arntz, Helmut.
Proposition pour l'organisation de la documentation en Tunisie—(mission) 4–17 décembre 1972. July 1973. 20p., tables.

Mission report providing suggestions for setting up a national information system in Tunisia—describes the proposed structure for this information service and the resulting requirements for information science training; gives recommendations for establishing the relevant instructional programme for documentation training and library training; examines curriculum development in library science and mentions the existing information network.

UNESCO DOC. CODE: 2947/RMO.RD/DBA; MICROFICHE: 73fr0285. (Restricted).

19. Ashworth, Wilfred; Francis, Simon.
Report to King Abdulaziz University on library services, 1975. 34p.

20. Aubrac, Jean Pierre.
La création et le développement d'une unité de documentation: Centre arabe d'étude sur les zones arides et les terres fermes (ACSAD)—(mission) 30 May 1983. 33p., illus.

Keywords: documentation centres; information/library development; agricultural research; research centres; arid zones; agricultural libraries; Arab countries; Syrian AR—regional cooperation; information/library co-operation; information processing; library collections; library automation; library services.
Identifiers: Arab Centre for the Studies of Arid Zones and Dry Lands (Syria), Unité de documentation.

UNESCO DOC. CODE: FMR/PGI/83/127; FMR/PGI/83/127A; RP/1981-83/5/10.1/03/Rapport technique. MICROFICHE: 83fr0160. (Restricted).

21. Aziz, S.M.
Establishment of a microfilm section at the King Abdul Aziz University, Jeddah: Saudi Arabia—(mission) December 1972-February 1973. April 1973.

Mission report on the establishment of a microfilm section in one of the university libraries in Saudi Arabia: the university of King Abdul Aziz in Jeddah, so as to preserve the library collections of other libraries in the country—evaluates requirements for microform equipment and occupational qualifications of the staff.

UNESCO DOC. CODE: 2898/RMO.RD/DBA; FR/UNDP/ Consultant. MICROFICHE: 73fr0236. (Restricted).

22. Badr, Ahmad.
Proposal for establishing the Department of Information and Library Services at Kuwait University. Kuwait: Kuwait University, 1974 (mimeographed).

The Bibliography 33

23. Barganier, Elhura.
    (*School library program in Libya*)—end of tour report. August 1959. 8p.
    USOM/TOICA-A-178, Aug. 8, 1959.

24. Barlag, T.
    Science and technology policy, planning and management in the Sudan—(mission) August 1976. 39p.

    Mission report giving an overall assessment of science policy and science planning in the Sudan, including reference to its scientific research—notes the need for a management information system and data base for planning and science budgeting, and an organized approach to the transfer of technology; deals with such related questions as natural resources, standardization, computer applications and the manpower needs for scientific personnel and technical personnel; mentions further research and development programmes, and refers to the role of the national research council in these programmes.

    UNESCO DOC. CODE: FMR/SC/STP/76/237 (UNDP) Prov.; UNDP/SUD/75/005/End-of-assignment report. MICROFICHE: 77fr0034.

25. Barnett, Stanley A.; Emmerson, Harold G.; Sharify, Nasser.
    Book production, importation and distribution in Turkey; a study of needs with recommendations within the context of social and economic development. Oyster Bay, N.Y.: State University of New York, International Studies and World Affairs, December 1966. 77p.
    U.S.A.I.D. CONTRACT NO. AID/CSd-1199.

26. Barnett, Stanley A.; Brown, Emerson L.; Frase, Robert W.; Hurst, Kenneth T.; Neumann, Peter H.; Thut, I.N.
    Books as tools for Turkish national growth; a survey and evaluation of the book industry in Turkey. Chicago: Wolf Management Engineering Co., 1965. 245p.
    U.S.A.I.D. CONTRACT NO. AID/CSd-681.

27. Barnett, Stanley A.; Brown, Emerson L.; Frase, Robert W.; Hurst, Kenneth T.; Neumann, Peter H.; Thut, I.N.

Books as tools for national growth and development; a case study of the use of books in Turkey. Chicago: Wolf Management Engineering Co., 1965. 216p.

U.S.A.I.D. CONTRACT NO. CSD-1162 GTS PN-AAE-264.

28. Barnett, Stanley A.; Brown, Emerson L.; Byrd, Cecil K.; Chevalier, H.F.; Dandison, B.G.; Gottleib, H.J.; Thomas, R.M.
Developmental book activities and needs in Indonesia, prepared for the U.S. Agency for International Development. New York: Wolf Management Services, June 1967. 232p.

U.S.A.I.D. CONTRACT NO. CSD-1162 GTS PN-AAE-263.

29. Barnett, Stanley A.
Planning and documentation assistance assignment in Djakarta, January 14–February 7, 1968. New York: Wolf Management Services. 35p., appendices.

U.S.A.I.D. CONTRACT NO. AID/ea-26.

30. Bartram, A.W.
Investigatory mission to Abu Dhabi in respect of the establishment of an audio-visual centre: United Arab Emirates—(mission) 23 July–3 August 1974. October 1974. 18p. (in various pagings), incl. bibl.

Mission report on the establishment of an audiovisual resource centre in Abu Dhabi, United Arab Emirates—discusses the background of the project and stages of its implementation; gives recommendations on the choice of audiovisual aids to be used by the Centre and the appointment of the staff.

UNESCO DOC. CODE: 3088/RMO.RD/ESM. MICROFICHE: 75fr0013. (Restricted).

31. Basset, Alice.
Étude de faisabilité d'un Centre national de documentation scientifique et technique: Sénégal—(mission) 4 novembre–1er décembre 1974. April 1975. 38p. (in various pagings), incl. bibl.

Mission report presenting a feasibility study for the establishment of a national documentation centre in Senegal to deal with scientific information—reviews the present situation and estimates future information user needs; mentions regional co-operation in scientific information in French speaking Africa; outlines documentation/library administration for the proposed information/service and its documentation/library personnel needs.

UNESCO DOC. CODE: 3160/RMO.RD/STD. MICROFICHE: 75fr0071.

32. Battu, Daniel Pierre; Rose, John B.
Telecommunication services for the transfer of information and data: Indonesia—(mission) 31 October 1982. 91p., illus., maps.

Keywords: telecommunication; information transfer; data transmission; informatics; Indonesia—communication technology; communication networks; telecommunication links; computer networks; data bases; information services; information user needs; communication policy; regional co-operation; South East Asia. **Identifiers:** National Packet Switching Network (Indonesia). PACKSATNET: Packet Satellite Data Network.

UNESCO DOC. CODE: FMR/PGI/82/166; RP/1981–83/5/10.1/03/ Technical report. MICROFICHE: 83fr0007.

33. Bekény, I.
Mali: réorganisation des archives, novembre–decembre 1969. Paris: Unesco, 1970. 17p.

UNESCO DOC. CODE: 2231/BMS.RD/DBA.

34. Bell, L.
Sierra Leone: organization of national archives, January 1966. Paris: Unesco, 1966. 23p.

35. Benson, Gregory.
Study of the present and projected activities of the Centre for Educational Research and Development, operated by the Lebanese Ministry of Education: Lebanon—(mission) 6 May 1981. 31p.

Keywords: educational research; research centres; educational information; dissemination of information; information/library planning; information services; Lebanon—administrative structure; on-line information systems; bibliographic services; bibliographic description; data bases; information/library personnel;

library training. **Identifiers:** Centre for Educational Research and Development (Lebanon).

UNESCO DOC. CODE: FMR/PGI/OPS/81/225 (SP); SP/413/LEB/3042/Technical report. MICROFICHE: 81fr0215. (Restricted).

36. Bernard, Hugh Y.
Report on law librarian's visit to Kabul, Afghanistan. Washington, D.C.: George Washington University, National Law Center, n.d. 27p.

Summarizes activities of visiting expert in Kabul; describes current state of Western language materials in Afghanistan and makes recommendations concerning acquisitions, their organization, and the general administration of a Western-oriented law library.

Keywords: Afghanistan–education; law; law library.

U.S.A.I.D. CONTRACT NO. AID/CM/ASIA-c-73-32; project 306-11-790-123. DOC. NO. B 306012300 5101 Undifferentiated Report (MICROFICHE: not available).

37. Bernier, Gaston.
La Bibliothèque de l'Institut africain de développement économique et de planification—(mission): évaluation et recommendations. August 1982. 14p.

Keywords: information/library development; scientific libraries; information systems evaluation; Africa—library collections; information/library operations; library services; information/library management. **Identifiers:** Institut africain de développement économique et de planification (Senegal), Bibliothèque.

UNESCO DOC. CODE: FMR/PGI/82/141; RP/1981–83/5/10.1/03/Rapport de mission. MICROFICHE: 82fr0116. (Restricted).

38. Berntsson, Ragnhild.
Library services for the visually handicapped: Malaysia—(mission) 30 September 1980. 18p.

Keywords: library services; blind; libraries for the blind; information/library facilities; Malaysia.

UNESCO DOC. CODE: FMR/PGI/80/166; RP/1979–80/5/10.1/05/Technical report. MICROFICHE: 81fr0016. (Restricted).

39. Blaquière, Henri.
Enseignement de l'archivistique à l'École des sciences de l'information: Maroc—(mission) 3 June 1980. 22p., incl. bibl.

    Keywords: archive science training; Morocco—information science training; teaching methods; university curriculum; curriculum development. **Identifiers:** École des sciences de l'information (Morocco).

    UNESCO DOC. CODE: FMR/PGI/OPS/80/230 (UNDP); UNDP/MOR/74/003/Rapport technique. MICROFICHE: 80fr0130.

40. Blaustin, Albert P.
    African law libraries, a survey of current needs: a report of the Project for the Staffing of African Institutions of Legal Education and Research (SAILER). Rutgers Law School, South Jersey Division, 15 August 1964.

41. Blaustin, Albert P.
    African law libraries, Kenya–Uganda–Zambia; a report to SAILER. August 1970.

42. Blaustin, Albert P.
    Preliminary and cursory observations on law library needs in Africa. 18 September 1963.

43. Bonny, Harold V.
    Report on school library service of Ministry of Education. Kuwait: Education Department, School Libraries Section, 1959, (mimeographed).

44. Borsa, Ivan.
    Development and modernization of the Basbakanlik Arsir: Turkey—(mission) 31 October 1980. 12p.

    Keywords: national archives; archive development; archive planning; Turkey—archive science training; archive records; archive legislation. **Identifiers:** Basbakanlik Archives (Turkey).

    UNESCO DOC. CODE: FMR/PGI/80/171; RP/1979–80/5/10.1/05/Technical report. MICROFICHE: 81fr0008. (Restricted).

45. Boulinier, G.
Le Centre national de documentation et de recherches: Les Comores—(mission) 30 June 1979. 46p., illus., incl. bibl.

Keywords: information/library development; documentation centre; research libraries; Comoros—information/library legislation; information/library resources; information/library facilities; information/library personnel; acquisition policy; library buildings. **Identifiers:** Centre national de documentation et de recherches (Comoros).

UNESCO DOC. CODE: FMR/PGI/79/158; PP/1977–78/5.1.5/ Rapport technique. MICROFICHE: 80fr0039. (Restricted).

46. Bousso, Amadou Alassane.
La Formation des bibliothécaires et le développement des bibliothèques universitaires en Afrique: pays francophones—(mission) 31 July 1980. 206p. (in various pagings).

Keywords: university libraries; library training; information/library personnel; information/library development; French speaking Africa—library collections; information users; library services; information/library budgets; library equipment; information/library co-operation; information/library statistics; library buildings; questionnaires; Algeria; Benin PR; Burundi; Congo PR; Ivory Coast; Gabon; Upper Volta; Madagascar DR; Mali; Morocco; Mauritius; Mauritania; Niger; Central African Republic; Cameroon UR; Rwanda; Senegal; Chad; Togo; Tunisia; Zaire.

UNESCO DOC. CODE: FMR/PGI/80/151; AUPELF/UNESCO/ RP/1975–76/4.22.3/1977–78/5.14.3/Rapport technique. MICROFICHE: 80fr0181. (Restricted).

47. Brawne, Michael.
Design of a central library for rare books, San'a: Yemen Arab Republic—(mission) 23 March–12 April 1978. August 1978. 26p., illus., plans.

Keywords: rare books; manuscripts; library buildings; building design; building costs; Yemen AR.

UNESCO DOC. CODE: FMR/BEP/PGI/78/133; RP/1977–78/ 5.13.8/Assignment report. MICROFICHE: 79fr0115. (Restricted).

48. Brawne, Michael.
Design of PASTIC (Pakistan Science and Technology Information Centre) in Islamabad—(mission) 2–27 August 1977. 19 December 1977. 18p. (in various pagings), illus., plans.

Mission report on the building design of a library building for a documentation centre and information service dealing with scientific information in Pakistan, providing detailed plans and an estimate of building costs.

Keywords: building design; library buildings; documentation centre; information services; scientific information; Pakistan; building costs. **Identifiers:** Pakistan Scientific and Technological Information Centre.

UNESCO DOC. CODE: FMR/PGI/77/273 (UNDP); UNDP/PAK/75/064/End-of-assignment report. MICROFICHE: 78fr0104. (Restricted).

49. Breton, Jean Marie.
Centre de documentation et d'information sur le développement: Liban—(mission) 10 janvier–9 mai 1975. Résultats et recommendations du project. 29 August 1975. 45p.

Mission report on the establishment and role of a documentation centre on development planning in the central government of Lebanon, namely the Ministry of Planning—describes present documentation/library operations and documentation/library facilities, and makes recommendations for their reorganization for filling information user needs; also recommends a central collection of official publications.

UNESCO DOC. CODE: FMR/COM/DND/75/216 (UNDP); UNDP/LEB/71/522/Rapport final. MICROFICHE: 76fr0047. (Restricted).

50. Brillant, Louis G.
Perfectionnement d'un service de documentation et d'études à l'Assemblée Nationale du Cameroon—(mission) 10 novembre–18 décembre 1974. January 1975. 51p. (in various pagings).

Mission report on the documentaton centre for the central government in Cameroon UR—discusses library equipment and the distribution of documentation/library personnel; considers the reference service being offered by the centre, its acquisitions policy and its archive administration.

UNESCO DOC. CODE: PNUD/CMR/72/007. MICROFICHE: 76fr0041. (Restricted).

51. Brown, Emerson L.; Naibert, Zane E.; Sharify, Nasser; Watts, Franklin.
Book production, importation, and distribution in Pakistan; a study of needs with recommendations within the context of social and economic development. Oyster Bay, N.Y.: State University of New York, International Studies and World Affairs, December 1966. 120p.

U.S.A.I.D. CONTRACT NO. AID/CSd-1199.

52. Cade, Joseph A.
Science policy and planning of research: Iran—(mission) March 1972. April 1973. 64p., charts, tables.

Mission report making recommendations to the Institute for Research Planning, Science and Education on science policy and research planning in Iran—stresses the need to establish research priorities; examines evaluation methods; considers that industrialization should be based on technological innovation; refers to requirements in scientific personnel and recommends the setting up of a documentation centre, preferably with computerized documentation.

UNESCO DOC. CODE: 2899/RMO.RD/SPI; FR/UNDP/Consultant. MICROFICHE: 73fr0217. (Restricted).

53. Carbone, Salvatore.
Formation archivistique à la Faculté d'information et de documentation de l'Université libanaise et organisation du dépôt de préarchivage—(mission) 31 July 1979. 33p.

Keywords: archive science training; archive development; national archives; Lebanon—archive administration; archive legislation; training courses; archive personnel; archive facilities.
Identifiers: Centre des archives nationales (Liban). Université libanaise, Faculté d'information et de documentation.

UNESCO DOC. CODE: FMR/PGI/79/172; RP/1979–80/5/10.1/ Rapport technique. MICROFICHE: 80fr0007. (Restricted).

54. *Centre for Statistical Data and Educational Documentation, Riyadh*: Saudi Arabia—(mission). Project findings and recommendations. 30 September 1982. 11p.

Keywords: educational statistics; educational documentation; Saudi Arabia—data processing; educational personnel; institution building. **Identifiers:** Centre for Statistical Data and Eductional Documentation, Riyadh (Saudi Arabia).

UNESCO DOC. CODE: FMR/ST/82/258 (UNDP); UNDP/SAU/74/004/Terminal report. MICROFICHE: 83fr0073. (Restricted).

55. *Centre national de documentation du Maroc*—(mission). Résultats et recommendations du project. 28 July 1976. 62p. (in various pagings), map.

Mission report describing the development of a national documentation centre to provide information services dealing with technical and scientific information in Morocco—outlines the documentation/library administration of the centre; mentions a thesaurus compilation for use in information retrieval; describes the work of the reference service and other documentation/library operations; refers to the introduction of computerized documentation to connect the centre to an international information system.

UNESCO DOC. CODE: FMR/CC/DBA/76/233 (UNDP); UNDP/MOR/71/538/Rapport final. MICROFICHE: 77fr0001. (Restricted).

56. *Centre national de documentation scientifique et technique*: Sénégal—(mission) 13 February 1979. 48p., illus.

Keywords: scientific information; national information system; documentation centre; Senegal—information/library personnel; information network; information user needs; information/library development; computer software; computer programming. **Identifiers:** Centre national de documentation scientifique et technique (Senegal). ISIS.

UNESCO DOC. CODE: FMR/PGI/79/212 (UNDP); UNDP/SEN/75/003/Rapport final. MICROFICHE: 80fr0026. (Restricted).

57. *Centre national de planification de la recherche scientifique et technologique*: Sénégal—(mission). Rapport sur les résultats du project.

July 1974. 35p. (in various pagings), illus.

Mission report evaluating a national research centre for research management and planning of scientific research in Senegal—presents recommendations for the training of research workers and for developing scientific potential and research priorities for research and development projects; considers information transfer from abroad and computer applications to scientific information; includes a discussion on the fourth national development plan for science and technology, 1973–7 and refers to fellowships.

UNESCO DOC. CODE: SEN/70/513. MICROFICHE: 74fr0158. (Restricted).

58. *Centre of information and exploitation of scientific and technical documentation concerning the natural resources of the Niger River Basin*: Niger River Commission (Cameroon, Chad, Dahomey, Guinea, Ivory Coast, Mali, Niger, Nigeria and Upper Volta)—(mission). Report on project results; conclusions and recommendations. August 1972. 31p.

Mission report on a project of data collection on the natural resources of the Niger river basin, involving interdisciplinary research with consultants in various fields–recommends a wider distribution of the Centre's abstracting and indexing service in co-operation with FAO, which should be prepared with a view to introducing computerized documentation; emphasizes the necessity for complete bilingualism in the work of the documentation centre.

UNESCO DOC. CODE: INT/UNESCO/UNDP REG.198. MICROFICHE: 73fr0051. (Restricted).

59. *Centre régional de formation d'archivists, Dakar*: Regional—(mission). Résultats et recommendations du project. 31 December 1976. 37p. (in various pagings).

Mission report on the establishment in Senegal of a regional training centre for archive science training for French speaking Africa; describes the administration of the centre which functions as a section of an established documentation/library school—discusses student selection, the academic teaching personnel and the centre's educational programmes; outlines the university curriculum offered and provides some educational statistics including those on enrolment.

UNESCO DOC. CODE: FMR/CC/DBA/76/271 (UNDP); UNDP/RAF/69/517/Rapport final. MICROFICHE: 77fr0029. (Restricted).

60. Chambellant, S.
Étude des termes de référence d'un système d'information scientifique et technologique au Cameroun. Unesco, 1975.

61. Chandler, George.
Tunisie: développement des bibliothèques. Paris: Unesco, 1964. 43p.
UNESCO DOC. CODE: PP/Tun/CUa/3.

62. Chari, N.R.
Libya: organization of photographic and film archives, December 1967–May 1968. Paris: Unesco, 1968. 19p.
UNESCO DOC. CODE: 901-BMS.RD/DBA.

63. Charlick, Robert B.
Planning and evaluating information and study functions for the Niamey Productivity Project. Lagos: U.S.A.I.D. Bureau for Africa, 1977. 62p.

Keywords: AID; Information; Information Centers; Projects; Research; Villages; Niger.

DOC. NO.: PN-AAF-578.

64. Charron, Janine.
Documentation évènementielle: la pratique de l'indexation au Centre de documentation nationale, Tunis: Tunisie—(mission) 30 June 1979. 84p., illus.

Keywords: documentation centre; abstracting and indexing service; indexing; Tunisia—classification/thesaurus system; thesaurus compilation; methodology; monolingual thesauri; information retrieval; evaluation; guides. **Identifiers:** Centre de documentation nationale (Tunisia).

UNESCO DOC. CODE: FMR/PGI/79/133; RP/1977–78/5.13.4/ Rapport de mission. MICROFICHE: 79fr0215. (Restricted).

44   *The Bibliography*

65. Childs, William M.
    University textbook program component of the university instructional materials and libraries project; final report and concept paper. Academy for Educational Development, Inc., December 1977. 1V.
    U.S.A.I.D. CONTRACT NO. AID/afr-e-1131.

66. Chonez, A.
    Liban: Centre national de documentation pour le développement, 10 juillet–13 août 1968. Paris: Unesco, 1968. 82p.

67. Contini-Allemand, Vittoria.
    Atelier de restauration à la Bibliothèque centrale de l'Université d'Istanbul: Turquie—(mission) 31 August 1979. 20p., illus., inc. bibl.

    Keywords: university libraries; laboratories; restoration; manuscripts; Turkey—conservation techniques; binding; laboratory equipment. **Identifiers:** University of Istanbul, Central Library.

    UNESCO DOC. CODE: FMR/PGI/79/178; PP/1977–78/5.1.5/ Rapport technique. MICROFICHE: 80fr0018. (Restricted).

68. Cooper, Michael D.
    Automation in the National Bibliographic and Scientific Computer Centre: Arab Republic of Egypt—(mission) 26 May 1983. 11p.

    Keywords: library automation; computer centres; national libraries; Egypt—computer software; systems analysis. **Identifiers:** General Egyptian Book Organization, National Bibliographic and Scientific Computer Centre.

    UNESCO DOC. CODE: FMR/PGI/83/125; PP/1981–83/5/10.1/ 05/Technical report. MICROFICHE: 83fr0098. (Restricted).

69. Cooper, Michael D.
    Automation in the National Library of Egypt: The Arab Republic of Egypt—(mission) 18 June 1981. 7p.

    Keywords: national libraries; library automation; on-line information systems; information/library planning; Egypt. **Identifiers:** National Library (Egypt).

    UNESCO DOC. CODE: FMR/PGI/OPS/81/231 (SA); SA/ARE/ 30.30/Assignment report. MICROFICHE: 81fr0172. (Restricted).

70. *Co-operation with Garyounis University*: the Socialist People's Libyan Arab Jamahiriya—(mission) 29 March–5 April 1978. 10 April 1978. 52p. (in various pagings).

Keywords: universities; educational administrative structure; educational priority areas; university libraries; educational costs; educational assistance; Libyan AR. **Identifiers:** Garyounis University (Libyan AR). Unesco—Relations with Member States.

UNESCO DOC. CODE: FMR/CAB/78/215 (FIT); FIT/ /9306/Technical report. MICROFICHE: 79fr0098. (Restricted).

71. Creasey, John C.
The collection and use of research project information: The Democratic Republic of the Sudan—(mission) 14 June 1982. 43p., illus., incl. bibl.

Keywords: research projects; data collection; information use; information services; Sudan—research registers; research and development; science budgets; science planning. **Identifiers:** National Council for Research (Sudan). Scientific Statistics Unit (Sudan). National Documentation Centre (Sudan).

UNESCO DOC. CODE: FMR/PGI/82/121; RP/1981–83/5/10.1/ 03/Technical report. MICROFICHE: 82fr0114.

72. Creasey, John C.
Development of the national register of research: Democratic Republic of the Sudan—(mission) 31 October 1983. 66p., illus., incl. bibl.

Keywords: research registers; research projects; scientific information; data collection; methodology; Sudan—editing; classification systems; indexing; questionnaires; subject headings; thesauri. **Identifiers:** National Council for Research (Sudan). National Documentation Centre (Sudan).

UNESCO DOC. CODE: FMR/PGI/83/173; RP/1981–83/5/10.1/ 03/Assignment report. MICROFICHE: 83fr0176. (Restricted).

73. Crisp, J.B.; Schyfsma, E.; Kennedy, P.J.; Mackenzie, A.G.; Kingston, J.; Clearhill, E.
Faculty of Science, University of Qatar—(mission) 4 August 1978. 274p., illus., plan.

Keywords: science education; university curriculum; university libraries; information/library development; Qatar—marine biology; biology education; geology education; chemistry education; physics education; computer science education; computer applications; informatics; scientific information; educational facilities; academic teaching personnel. **Identifiers:** University of Qatar, Faculty of Science.

UNESCO DOC. CODE: FMR/SC/OPS/78/240 (FIT); FIT/9712/QAT/90/Technical report. MICROFICHE: 79fr0074. (Restricted).

74. Delmas, Bruno.

    La formation des archivistes: propositions pour un programme d'enseignement à l'école des sciences de l'information de Rabat (ESI): Maroc—(mission) 6–19 décembre 1976. 14 February 1978. 40p., incl. bibl.

    Keywords: archive science training; information science training; Morocco—archive facilities; archive personnel; archive development; curriculum guides; information/library schools. **Identifiers:** École des sciences de l'information de Rabat (Morocco).

    UNESCO DOC. CODE: FMR/CC/DBA/78/204 (UNDP); UNDP/MOR/74/003/Rapport technique. MICROFICHE: 79fr0013. (Restricted).

75. Delmas, Bruno F.

    La formation des archivistes: propositions pour un programme d'enseignement à l'École des sciences de l'information de Rabat: Maroc—(mission) 6–19 décembre 1976. 19 October 1977. 72p. (in various pagings), incl. bibl.

    Mission report on archive science training at an information science training school in Morocco—outlines the country's needs for archivists and existing archive facilities; includes detailed curriculum guides and provides a copy of the educational programme of this documentation/library school.

    Keywords: archive science training; information science training; Morocco—archivists; archive facilities; curriculum guides; educational programmes; information/library schools. **Identifiers:** École des sciences de l'information (Morocco).

    UNESCO DOC. CODE: FMR/CC/DBA/77/260 (UNDP) (Prov.);

UNDP/MOR/74/003/Rapport technique. MICROFICHE: 78fr0039. (Restricted).

76. Delmas, Bruno F.
Reconstitution des archives administratives—developpement d'un système national: Liban—(mission) 2–14 mai 1977. 18 July 1977. 24p., illus., map.

Mission report presenting an evaluation of the damage caused to the national archives by the civil war in Lebanon—reviews the state of archive documents in public administration and the government services; underlines the role of international co-operation in reconstructing the archive collection.

Keywords: evaluation; damage; national archives; civil war; Lebanon—archive records; public administration; government service, international co-operation.

UNESCO DOC. CODE: FMR/BEP/PGI/77/173; RP/1977–78/5.1.3/Rapport technique. MICROFICHE: 78fr0072. (Restricted).

77. Desroches-Noblecourt, Christiane.
Création d'un centre de documentation 'Campagne archéologique pour Carthage': Tunisie—(mission) décembre 1974. April 1975. 8p.

Mission report advising on the establishment of a documentation centre in archaeology, especially related to the archaeological excavations being undertaken within the framework of the Save Carthage Campaign in Tunisia—refers to the classification of archaeological objects from the ancient city, and the documentation/library facilities required.

UNESCO DOC. CODE: 3172/RMO.RD/CLP. MICROFICHE: 75fr0078. (Restricted).

78. Dethoor, Jean Marc; Groboillot, Jean Louis.
Advisory mission on preparation of a contract with Al-Kabir Trading Co. for delivery of a microform system: Saudi Arabia—(mission) 31 March 1981. 13p. (in various pagings).

Keywords: microform equipment; computer output microform; information systems; Saudi Arabia. **Identifiers:** Saudi Arabia. Ministry of Foreign Affairs, Computer Control Microfilm Search System.

UNESCO DOC. CODE: FMR/PGI/OPS/81/216 (UNDP); UNDP/

SAU/80/011/Assignment report. MICROFICHE: 81fr0139. (Restricted).

79. Dethoor, Jean Marc; Groboillot, Jean Louis.
Preliminary discussions for the installation of a microfilm system for the Ministry of Foreign Affairs: Saudi Arabia—(mission) 31 December 1980. 12p.

Keywords: computer output microform; information systems; information processing automation; government departments; Saudi Arabia—computer software; computer hardward; information/library facilities; information/library administration. **Identifiers:** Computer Control Microfilm Search System (Saudi Arabia).

UNESCO DOC. CODE: FMR/DTP/80/278 (UNDP); UNDP/ SAU/80/009/Assignment report. MICROFICHE: 81fr0084. (Restricted).

80. Dethoor, Jean Marc; Groboillot, Jean Louis.
Selection of a microform system for the Ministry of Foreign Affairs of the Kingdom of Saudi Arabia—(mission) 1980. 63p., illus.

Keywords: computer output microform; information systems; information processing automation; information/library planning; information services; government departments; Saudi Arabia—data bases; project design; computer personnel. **Identifiers:** Saudi Arabia. Ministry of Foreign Affairs, Computer Control Microfilm Search System.

UNESCO DOC. CODE: FMR/DTP/80/241 (UNDP); UNDP/ SAU/80/009/Technical report. MICROFICHE: 80fr0182. (Restricted).

81. *Development of the national education programme*: Indonesia—(mission). Project findings and recommendations. 6 October 1978. 42p., incl. bibl.

Keywords: educational programmes; educational development; educational planning; Indonesia—educational information; data collection; data processing; educational administration; educational management; computer applications; curriculum development; teacher training; educational technology; book development. information/library development; non-formal education; educational innovations; evaluation of education; educational personnel training; fellowship.

UNESCO DOC. CODE: FMR/ED/OPS/78/252 (UNDP); UNDP/INS/71/537/Terminal report. MICROFICHE: 79fr0031. (Restricted).

82. Diamond, A.I.
Establishment of a National Archives Service: Afghanistan—(mission) November–December 1974. February 1975. 70p., illus.

Mission report on the setting-up of a national archives collection in Afghanistan—describes the present practice of records management and discusses the proposed building design for the collection, including fire protection measures; outlines problems of archive administration, a programme for archive development and the archive legislation necessary for proper control of public records, includes recommendations for archive science training.

UNESCO DOC. CODE: 3129/RMO.RD/DBA. MICROFICHE: 75fr0080.

83. Dickinson, Asa Don.
Report on work at the Punjab University Library, October 1915 to July 1916. Lahore: July 13, 1916.

84. Djoleto, S.A. Amu.
Developing the textbook industry and the National Book Development Council: Sierra Leone—(mission) 15 September 1982. 39p., incl. bibl.

Keywords: book industry; textbook production; book development; Sierra Leone—publishing; book distribution; government organizations; administrative structure; professional associations. **Identifiers:** National Book Development Council (Sierra Leone).

UNESCO DOC. CODE: FMR/COM/LPE/82/153; RP/1981–83/4/3.5/07/Technical report. MICROFICHE: 82fr0124. (Restricted).

85. *Documentation and Analysis Centre for the Niger River Commission*: Regional—(mission). Project findings and recommendations. 31 December 1976. 17p. (in various pagings).

Mission report on the establishment of a documentation centre and information service in the field of scientific information in

50 The Bibliography

Niger for the Niger River Commission Member States; covers hydrological research on the natural resources of the Niger River Basin—outlines the documentation/library administration and activities of the centre, with special reference to the dissemination of information and the development of an abstracting and indexing service; also recommends the creation of a regional information network for information exchange and the exchange of publications.

UNESCO DOC. CODE: FMR/SC/OPS/76/276 (UNDP); UNDP/RAF/70/198/Terminal report. MICROFICHE: 77fr0038. (Restricted).

86. *Documentation Centre—Ministry of National Planning*: Somalia—(mission). Project findings and recommendations. 26 August 1982. 46p.

    Keywords: information/library development; information services; library services; documentation centres; Somalia—information user needs; government libraries; acquisition policy; information/library operations; library training; information/library co-operation; national information systems; information systems evaluation. **Identifiers:** Somalia. Ministry of National Planning, Documentation Centre.

    UNESCO DOC. CODE: FMR/PGI/OPS/82/253 (UNDP); UNDP/SOM/76/009/Terminal report. MICROFICHE: 83fr0024. (Restricted).

87. Donovan, David G.
    Report on Pakistan's information transfer system, 16 June–13 July 1974. 1974. 54p.

    Keywords: librarians; libraries; national planning; personnel development; professional personnel; Pakistan.

    U.S.A.I.D. CONTRACT NO. AID/ASIA-C-1088. DOC. NO. PN-AA F-352.

88. Downs, Report B.
    The Kabul University Library: an evaluation of its present status and recommendations for its growth and development, together with proposals for the improvement of other libraries in Kabul. Wyoming University, August 1963. 60p.

89. Dunchein, Michel.
Planning and equipment of the national archives building: Malaysia—(mission) November 1971. February 1972. 23p. (in various pagings), plans.

Mission report on the archive planning and archive facilities of the National Archives in Kuala Lumpur, Malaysia—sets out basic requirements and building standards necessary to ensure good working conditions and functioning of the archives repository.

UNESCO DOC. CODE: 2615/RMO.RD/DBA. MICROFICHE: 73fr0120.

90. Dulong, Aubert.
Situation et perspectives de l'information scientific et technique: Syrie—(mission), février-mars 1976. 30 June 1976. 52p., incl. bibl.

Mission report on the creation of a national documentation centre to deal with technical and scientific information in the Syrian AR, within the UNISIST framework—reviews the existing scientific libraries and information services in this field; discusses problems of documentation/library personnel, information user needs and documentation/library financing; considers the establishment of a national information network based on documentation/library co-operation; briefly mentions regional co-operation with other Arab States and relations with non-Arab countries.

UNESCO DOC. CODE: FMR/SC/STI/76/125; PP/1975-76/2.131.7/Rapport technique. MICROFICHE: 77fr0104. (Restricted).

91. Dunningham, A.G.W.
Indonesia: library development in Indonesia. Paris: Unesco, Expanded Programme of Technical Assistance, 1964. 25p.

UNESCO DOC. CODE: EPTA/Indoem/4.

92. Dunningham, A.G.W.; Patah, R.
Report on a survey and recommendations for the establishment of a national library for Indonesia. Djakarta: 1973.

93. Dye, Jerry W.
Final report on library affairs in Pakistan. Karachi: June 1965.

94. *École des sciences de l'information*: Maroc—(mission). Résultats et recommendations du project. 8 December 1981. 70p. (in various pagings), incl. bibl.

    Keywords: information science training; information/library schools; Morocco—enrolment; university curriculum; curriculum guides; examinations; academic teaching personnel; teaching methods; teaching materials; audiovisual materials; information/library resources; educational financing; educational planning. **Identifiers:** École des sciences de l'information (Morocco).

    UNESCO DOC. CODE: FMR/PGI/OPS/81/281 (UNDP); UNDP/MOR/74/003/Rapport final. MICROFICHE: 81fr0295.

95. Ede, J.R.
    Construction of a national archives building: Iraq—(mission) 30 June 1980. 41p., illus.

    Keywords: national archives; archive repositories; archive planning; building design; Iraq—archive equipment; archive science training; archive personnel; archive development; archive administration; archive records. **Identifiers:** National Centre of Archives (Iraq.)

    UNESCO DOC. CODE: FMR/PGI/80/124; PP/1979–80/10.1/ Technical report. MICROFICHE: 80fr0162. (Restricted).

96. *Educational Research Centre, University of Baghdad*: Iraq—(mission) 1 July 1973–31 December 1975. Project findings and recommendations. 25 February 1976. 20p. (in various pagings), incl. bibl.

    Mission report on a research centre for educational research at the University of Bagdad, Iraq—describes the objectives of this centre as assisting in quantitative and qualitative educational planning and in effecting changes in the educational system; considers the centre's activities for educational personnel training and research training, with mention of a programmed instruction course and an in-service training programme; describes the educational administration of the centre, its research programmes and its diffusion of educational documentation and information; also refers to educational evaluation studies and links with the decision making process.

UNESCO DOC. CODE: FMR/ED/TEP/76/206 (UNDP); UNDP/IRQ/72/006/Terminal report. MICROFICHE: 76fr0103. (Restricted).

97. *Educational Technology Centre, College of Education, Riyadh University* (previously known as Educational Research Centre): Saudi Arabia—(mission) 22 November 1977. 10p. (in various pagings).

Mission report on the establishment of an educational technology and audiovisual resource centre at Riyadh University in Saudi Arabia—describes the educational equipment of the centre and the training courses offered.

Keywords: educational technology; multimedia resources centres; universities; Saudi Arabia—educational equipment; training courses. **Identifiers:** Riyadh University, College of Education, Educational Technology Centre.

UNESCO DOC. CODE: FMR/ED/OPS/77/267 (UNDP/FIT); UNDP/SAU/71/008; FIT/9339/SAU/Terminal statement. MICROFICHE: 78fr0112. (Restricted).

98. Emmerson, Harold G.; Lancour, Harold A.; Naibert, Zane E.; Serviss, Trevor K.
Book production, importation and distribution in Iran; a study of needs with recommendations within the context of social and economic development. Oyster Bay, N.Y.: State University of New York, International Studies and World Affairs, December 1966. 44p.

U.S.A.I.D. CONTRACT NO. AID/CSd-1199.

99. *Enseignement technique et professionnel*: services d'information et de documentation; etudes de cas, 1: Liban. 1980. 119p., illus.

UNESCO DOC. CODE: MICROFICHE: 80S0981.

100. Evans, Frank B.
Development of the archives and records management programme: Malaysia—(mission) 20 April 1982. 54p., incl. bibl.

Keywords: information/library management; archive records;

national archives; Malaysia—archive administration; records appraisal; information/library operations; information/library policy; questionnaires.

UNESCO DOC. CODE: FMR/PGI/82/110; RP/1981–83/5/10.1/03/Technical report. MICROFICHE: 82fr0064. (Restricted).

101. Eyre, John J.
Library development (NATIS); Republic of Afghanistan—(mission) 4 July–3 August 1976. 1 March 1977. 58p., map.

Mission report on documentation/library development in Afghanistan with emphasis on the development of public libraries within the framework of a national information system—reviews the present library service in the national library, university libraries and school libraries; deals with questions of library training and book production; briefly examines possibilities of computer applications to documentation/library operations; provides statistical data.

Keywords: information/library development; Afghanistan; public libraries; national information systems—library services; national libraries; university libraries; school libraries; library training; book production; computer applications; information/library operations; statistical data. **Identifiers:** NATIS.

UNESCO DOC. CODE: FMR/CC/DBA/77/115; PP/1975–76/4.221.4/Technical report. MICROFICHE: 78fr0027. (Restricted).

102. Faivre D'Arciev, B.
République populaire du Bénin: politique culturelle. Paris: Unesco, 1976. 67p.

UNESCO DOC. CODE: FMR/CCICD/76/117.

103. Faye, Bernard.
Construction d'un complexe documentaire Archives nationales—Bibliothèque nationale: Guinée—(mission) 1 June 1982, 44p., illus., plan.

Keywords: national archives; national libraries; library buildings; information/library development; Guinea—library stock; library equipment; sites; architecture; building design; information/library financing; archive repositories; archive legislation; information/library administration; climatic data. **Identifiers:**

Institut national de recherche et de documentation de Guinée. Bibliothèque nationale (Guinea). Archives nationales (Guinea).

UNESCO DOC. CODE: FMR/PGI/82/119; RP/1981-83/5/10.1/ 03/Rapport technique. MICROFICHE: 82fr0075.

104. Fayein, Claudie.
Rapport de mission en République Arabe du Yemen effectuée en vue d'établir un inventaire des ressources et des reconnaissance et à l'affirmation d'identité culturelle dans ce pays. 29 May 1980.

    Keywords: cultural identity; cultural resources; cultural needs; Yemen AR—cultural facilities; museums; libraries; handicrafts.

    UNESCO DOC. CODE: CC.80/WS/32. MICROFICHE: 80S1062.

105. Fegan, Ethel S.
Report on library needs in British West Africa. London: British Council, 1942. 15p.

106. FitzGerald, William A.
Instructional materials project in Libya: end of tour reports. [n.d.]

    U.S.A.I.D. CONTRACT NO. 670-11-690-038.

107. Flieder, F.
Bibliothèque nationale et archives générales; protection physique des manuscrits et des fonds d'archives: Tunisie—(mission) décembre 1973. February 1974. 6p.

    Mission report on problems of manuscript and book preservation at the national library and national archives of Tunisia.

    UNESCO DOC. CODE: 3016/RMO.RD/DBA. MICROFICHE: 74fr0096. (Restricted).

108. Flood, R.A.
Library development in the Gambia—report to the British Council. 1970.

109. Fodor, Michael.
Libraries and bibliographical services: assessment report. Karachi: Unesco Regional Reading Materials Centre, 1961. (Typewritten).

110. Fontvieille, Jean R.
 Création d'une infrastructure nationale des archives, des bibliothèques et de la documentation: Gabon—(mission) 30 November 1979. 103p., illus., plan.

 Keywords: information/library development; archive development; documentation; Gabon—national libraries; university libraries; scientific libraries; special libraries; documentation centre; public libraries; school libraries; information/library administration; information/library legislation; information/library personnel; cultural centres. **Identifiers:** Bibliothèque nationale (Gabon).

 UNESCO DOC. CODE: FMR/PGI/79/308; PP/1977-78/5.1.5/Rapport technique. MICROFICHE: 80fr0072. (Restricted).

111. Fontvieille, Jean R.
 Système national d'information Camerounais (SYNAICAM) — (mission) 23 février–13 mars 1976. 27 August 1976. 27p.

 Mission report on the development of a national information system in Cameroon UR within the framework of the NATIS Programme—provides an analysis of national documentation/library co-operation, including the national archives, the national library, the national library association and existing library services; stresses the need for promoting copyright deposit, preparing a national bibliography, and for improving the training of documentation/library personnel.

 UNESCO DOC. CODE: FMR/CC/DBA/76/140; PP/1975-76/4.221.4/Rapport technique. MICROFICHE: 77fr0123. (Restricted).

112. Forget, J.
 Organisation et formation des personnels en service dans le domaine de le documentation au Ministère des enseignements primaire et secondaire et dans les organismes sous tutelle: Algérie—(mission) août 1971. January 1972. 67p., tables.

 Mission report on the organization of educational documentation services of/or related to the central government, namely the Ministry of Primary Education and Secondary Education in Algeria in view of the centralization of these services within a single documentation centre—covers questions relating to classification, acquisitions policy, in-service training, etc.

UNESCO DOC. CODE: 2589/RMO.RD/EP. MICROFICHE: 73fr0009. (Restricted).

113. Francis, Simon.
Development of documentation and academic library services: Iraq—(mission) 3 November–30 December 1976. 31 December 1977. 51p., incl. bibl.

Mission report on documentation/library development in Iraq, with special reference to university libraries and information services in scientific information—reviews the present situation in academic libraries, outlining the documentation/library administration and describing the library stock and all documentation/library operations; discusses the scientific documentation centres and advocates the creation of a national information system for greater dissemination of information and information transfer.

Keywords: information/library development; Iraq; university libraries; information services; scientific information—academic libraries; information/library administration; library stock; information/library operations; documentation centre; national information systems; dissemination of information; information transfer.

UNESCO DOC. CODE: FMR/BEP/PGI/77/314; PP/1975-76/4.221.4/Technical report. MICROFICHE: 78fr0143.

114. Franklin Publications, Inc.
Books in the Republic of Guinea. January 1963. 19p.

115. Franklin Publications, Inc.
Educational books for the needs of Morocco: survey report and recommendations 1 August 1965. New York, 1965, (Mimeographed).

U.S.A.I.D. CONTRACT NO. AID/CSd-465.

116. Franz, E.G.
Formation archivistique: création d'un centre de formation des archivistes, des bibliothécaires et des documentalistes: Liban—(mission mars–avril 1974. June 1974. 32p.

Mission report on archive science training in Lebanon—describes the present system of archive administration and library training; recommends the establishment of a section for documentation training at the Institut d'information of the Lebanese University and includes curriculum for this as well as for a shorter refresher course.

UNESCO DOC. CODE: 3050/RMO.RD/DBA. MICROFICHE: 75fr0010. (Restricted).

117. *Future development of the University of Qatar*—(mission) 5–16 January 1978. Findings and recommendations. 16 March 1978. 110p., illus.

Keywords: universities; higher education; educational development; educational planning; Qatar—university curriculum; educational administrative structure; university libraries; multimedia resource centres; educational costs; university extension; school building and equipment; architecture; building costs; laboratories; enrolment. **Identifiers:** University of Qatar.

UNESCO DOC. CODE: FMR/ED/SC/78/209 (FIT). MICROFICHE: 79fr0026. (Restricted).

118. Gallal, A.M.
Historical survey of libraries in Libya up to the present time: report to Unesco. August 1972.

119. Gamaluddin, Ahmad.
University instructional materials project; library science consultant services. January 1978. 22p.

Keywords: libraries; universities; library science education—Egypt.

U.S.A.I.D. CONTRACT NO. AID/NE-c-1480; Project No. 263-0025. DOC. NO. PN-AAG-435.

120. Gelfand, Morris A.
Library education in Hacettepa University: Turkey—(mission) 18 November–13 December 1976. 15 February 1977. 34p., incl. bibl.

Mission report presenting an educational evaluation of a documentation/library school for library training at a university in Turkey—reviews the educational goals of the programme, its university curriculum, admission criteria and documentation/library facilities, provides educational statistics.

Keywords: evaluation of education; information/library schools; library training; universities; Turkey—educational goals; university curriculum; admission criteria; information/library facilities; educational statistics. **Identifiers:** Hacettepe University (Turkey), Dept. of Library Science.

UNESCO DOC. CODE: FMR/PGI/77/121; RP/1975–76/4.221.3/ Technical report. MICROFICHE: 77fr0161. (Restricted).

121. Gillet, Jean E.
Information de l'inventaire du potentiel scientifique et technique: Maroc—(mission) 24 May 1978. 79p.

Keywords: scientific potential; scientific information; data collection; scientific research; research and development; scientific personnel; questionnaires; Morocco—science financing; science policy; computer software. **Identifiers:** International Standard Nomenclature for Fields of Science and Technology (proposed).

UNESCO DOC. CODE: FMR/SC/STP/78/229 (UNDP); UNDP/ MOR/74/011/Rapport technique. MICROFICHE: 79fr0071. (Restricted).

122. Gillet, Jean E.
Politique scientifique et technologique-bases de données informatisées: Sénégal—(mission) janvier 1975–octobre 1977. 18 November 1977. 51p. (in various pagings), incl. bibl.

Mission report on the establishment of a data base in Senegal to deal with scientific information, especially that relevant to science policy and science planning—examines the role of the data bank in research planning and research and development; refers to an inventory on the country's scientific potential; also deals with aspects of data processing and science budgeting.

Keywords: data bases; Senegal; scientific information; science policy; science planning—data banks; research planning; reserch and development; inventories; scientific potential; data processing; science budgets.

UNESCO DOC. CODE: FMR/SC/STP/77/266 (UNDP); UNDP/ SEN/74/003/Rapport technique final. MICROFICHE: 78fr0134. (Restricted).

123. Gordon, John C.
Circulation of the printed media: Arab states—(mission) 29 May–24 June 1977. 5 May 1977. 34p.

Mission report on the international circulation of materials, specifically newspaper and exchange of publications between the Gulf states of Bahrain, Iraq, Kuwait, Oman (Sultanate), Qatar, Saudi Arabia and the United Arab Emirates—examines the present situation and national policy of each country concerning news flow, newspaper distribution and information exchange; discusses censorship requirements and transport problems.

Keywords: international circulation of materials; newspapers; exchange of publications; Gulf states; Bahrain; Iraq; Kuwait; Oman (Sultanate); Qatar; Saudi Arabia; United Arab Emirates—national policy; news flow; information exchange; censorship; transport.

UNESCO DOC. CODE: FMR/CC/DCS/148; RP/1975–76/4.131.1/ Technical report. MICROFICHE: 78fr0069. (Restricted).

124. Grasshoff, Klaus; Canzonier, Walter J.
Marine Sciences Centre, Lattakia: Syrian Arab Republic—(mission) 6–16 May 1978. October 1978. 53p., illus., plans.

Keywords: oceanographic research; research centres; scientific programmes; research programmes; Syrian AR—scientific personnel; physical oceanography; chemical oceanography; marine biology; marine geology; research ships; scientific information ; oceanographic laboratories; building design. **Identifiers:** Marine Sciences Centre, Lattakia (Syrian AR).

UNESCO DOC. CODE: FMR/SC/OCE/78/153; PP/1977–78/ 2.181.2/Technical report. MICROFICHE: 79fr0094. (Restricted).

125. Grieder, Elmer.
Ankara University, Faculty of Letters, Institute of Librarianship. (Report to) Members of the ALA Committee, 12 March 1956.

126. Grolier, Eric de.
Assistance à l'École des sciences de l'information: Maroc—(mission) 26 mars–26 juillet 1975. 31 December 1975. 26p., incl. bibl.

Mission report dealing with an information science training school in Morocco; describes the activities and curriculum development of this documentation/library school—considers its teaching methods, teaching materials and the nature of its students; also refers to the examinations given; discusses various problems concerning school libraries, with special reference to the Ecole des sciences de l'information, and provides recommendations on the future development of the school.

UNESCO DOC. CODE: FMR/COM/DND/75/252 (UNDP); UNDP/MOR/74/003/Rapport technique. MICROFICHE: 76fr0082. (Restricted).

127. Grolier, Eric de.
Centre national de documentation economique et sociale: Alger—(mission) 15 juin–14 juillet 1976. 24 November 1976. 62p.

Mission report on a documentation centre providing social science information and economic information as part of the national information system in Algeria—examines the present documentation/library operations; documentation/library administration and information services; briefly analyses the country's library resources in terms of library collections; discusses problems of documentation/library personnel; considers the national information policy and the need for international co-operation; includes documentation/library statistics.

UNESCO DOC. CODE: FMR/CC/DBA/76/163; RP/1975–76/4.221.2/Rapport technique. MICROFICHE: 77fr0067. (Restricted).

128. Grolier, Eric de.
Development of the National Documentation Centre: Hashemite Kingdom of Jordan—(mission) 15 February 1977. 67p. (in various pagings), incl. bibl.

Mission report on documentation/library development in Jordan, studying the actual situation of library services and advising on the development of a national documentation centre—provides an overall survey of human resources, natural resources, industrial production, social services and public finance in order to determine socio-economic factors important to the planning of a NATIS (National Information System); reviews the mass media and documentation/library facilities, stressing the need for an overall information policy and greater co-ordination to create a coherent information network; provides recommendations on the functions of the proposed documentation centre, mentioning centralized cataloguing, documentation/library planning and responsibility for a manpower policy concerning documentation/library personnel; provides statistical data.

Keywords: information/library development; Jordan; library services; documentation centre—surveys; human resources; natural resources; industrial production; social services; public finance; socio-economic factors; national information systems; mass media; information/library facilities; information/library policy; information/library networks; centralized cataloguing; information/library planning; manpower; information/library personnel; statistical data. **Identifiers:** National Documentation Centre (Jordan) (proposed). NATIS.

UNESCO DOC. CODE: FMR/PGI/77/123; PP/1975-76/4.221.4/ Technical report. MICROFICHE: 78fr0049.

129. Guénin, Jean Pierre.
Promotion du livre: République du Mali—(mission) 30 June 1979. 17p., illus.

Keywords: book development; textbook production; printing workshops; teacher training schools; Mali—printing equipment; offset; binding; photocomposition; printing paper; book production training. **Identifiers:** Institut pédagogique national (Mali), Imprimerie.

UNESCO DOC. CODE: FMR/CC/BCE/79/160; PP/1977-78/ 4.161.3/Rapport technique. MICROFICHE: 80fr0035. (Restricted).

130. Guinchat, Claire.
Centre de documentation et d'études sur le développement culturel: Tunisie—(mission) 31 May 1976. 33p., incl. bibl.

Mission report on the development of a documentation centre for providing information service on cultural development in Tunisia—discusses documentation/library operations and documentation/library personnel; examines its possible development into a regional centre for North Africa.

UNESCO DOC. CODE: FMR/CC/CD/76/123; RP/1975-76/ 3.321.5/Rapport technique. MICROFICHE: 77fr0091. (Restricted).

131. Guinchat, Claire.
Centre de documentation sur le développement culturel: Iran—(mission) 4 novembre–16 décembre 1973. April 1974. 48p., incl. bibl.

Mission report on the setting up of a documentation centre for cultural development in Iran—examines various documentation processes, with special emphasis on classification; stresses the need for documentation training and discusses the future of the centre with reference to regional co-operation; includes the classification system used.

UNESCO DOC. CODE: 3028/RMO.RD/SHC. MICROFICHE: 74fr0115. (Restricted).

132. Guinchat, Claire.
Centre d'études, de recherches et de documentation sur le développement culturel: Republique gabonaise—(mission) 7 juin–16 juillet 1976. 1976. 32p. (in various pagings), incl. bibl.

Mission report on documentation/library planning for the establishment of a documentation centre dealing with cultural research on cultural development in Gabon—assesses information user needs in view of the development of the country's cultural policy; discusses questions of documentation training; library training, information sources and information processing; includes brief notes on the documentation/library administration of the proposed centre.

UNESCO DOC. CODE: FMR/CC/CD/76/173; RP/1975-76/ 3.321.5/Rapport technique. MICROFICHE: 77fr0061. (Restricted).

133. Guran, M.; Sévenier, R.
Pour une politique nationale de l'informatique: Gabon—(mission) 30 November 1980. 61p. (in various pagings), illus., map.

Keywords: information/library policy; scientific information systems; information/library planning; information services; Gabon—scientific research; information/library personnel; information science training; information/library financing; private sector; public sector; information/library legislation; university curriculum; computer hardware; information processing automation. **Identifiers:** Association gabonaise d'informatique.

UNESCO DOC. CODE: FMR/SC/STP/80/187; RP/1979–80/2/03/ 2/4/3/08/Rapport technique. MICROFICHE: 81fr0060. (Restricted).

134. Gut, Christian.
Création d'un service national d'archives: Tchad—(mission) décembre 1972–février 1973. September 1973. 34p., tables.

Mission report on the establishment of a national archives in Chad for the deposit of central government and local government documents—discusses problems of physical location, legislation, recruitment, and archive science training for its personnel.

UNESCO DOC. CODE: 2974/RMO.RD/DBA. MICROFICHE: 74fr0040. (Restricted).

135. Gut, Christian.
Réorganisation des archives nationales: République Islamique de Mauritanie—(mission) 25 février–25 mars 1976. 10 July 1976. 20p. (in various pagings), maps.

Mission report on the reorganization of the national archives in Mauritania—examines existing archive legislation and discusses problems of physical location, archive administration, and archive science training.

UNESCO DOC. CODE: FMR/CC/DBA/76/137; PP/1975–76/ 4.221.4/Rapport technique. MICROFICHE: 77fr0002. (Restricted).

136. El-Haddidy, Bahaa.
Training of Egyptian information specialists: a multifaceted system approach, final report. Washington, D.C.: Catholic University of America, School of Library and Information Science, January 1982, xi, 222p.

Keywords: information systems; professional development; institution building; Egypt—training methods; participant training; curriculum development; training facilities; library science education; management training; information centres.

U.S. NATIONAL SCIENCE FOUNDATION CONTRACT NO. PASA NF/EGY/0016-7-77. DOC. NO. PN-AAP-016.

137. Hafenrichter, J.L.
University instructional materials project; inputs on library development, concepts paper. Washington, D.C.: U.S.A.I.D., Bureau for Development Support, Office of Development Information and Utilization, 1978. 23p.

Keywords: libraries; instructional materials; library science education; Egypt.

DOC. NO. PN-AAG-436.

138. Al-Hagrasy, Saad.
Documentation at the Ministry of Education: State of Qatar—(mission) 16 August 1982. 24p., incl. bibl.

Keywords: eductional documentation; information/library development; government educational bodies; Qatar—national information systems; information/library resources; information/library planning; library services. **Identifiers:** Qatar. Ministry of Education.

UNESCO DOC. CODE: FMR/ED/OPS/82/247 (FIT); FIT/900/QAT/14/Assignment report. MICROFICHE: 82fr0105.

139. Haider, Ali.
Development of school libraries; Uganda—(mission) 31 December 1978. 63p., map, incl. bibl.

Keywords: school libraries; information/library development; library services; information/library financing; Uganda—educational systems; book industry; teacher librarians; school librarians; library training; information/library operations; information use; reading guidance; curriculum development.

UNESCO DOC. CODE: FMR/BEP/PGI/78/172; RP/1977–78/5.1.3/Technical report. MICROFICHE: 79fr0123. (Restricted).

140. Hall, Hal O.
Libraries development program in Indonesia: end of tour reports. U.S.A.I.D. (n.d.)

141. Hamdy, Mohamed.
Gulf Vision System, Riyadh; a summary of the study on the feasibility of establishing a unit for the documentation of television

information and programmes within the Gulf Vision System in Riyadh. 8 February 1980. 8p., illus., plans.

Keywords: information services; documentation centres; television programmes; feasibility studies; Gulf States—film libraries; reference libraries. **Identifiers:** Gulf Vision System.

UNESCO DOC. CODE: CC.80/WS/3. MICROFICHE: 80S0752.

142. Hanley, Lawrence J.
Training course on book design and illustration: the Islamic Republic of Pakistan—(mission) 31 July 1981. 6p.

Keywords: book production training; illustration printing; training courses; Pakistan—curriculum development.

UNESCO DOC. CODE: FMR/CC/BCE/81/168; RP/1979–80/4/3/5/07/Assignment report. MICROFICHE: 81fr0174. (Restricted).

143. Harris, Philip.
Sierra Leone: book development report. Paris: Unesco, 1971. 45p.

UNESCO DOC. CODE: MCD/3939/1311.

144. Harrison, B.
Report on the development of national documentation and information services in Indonesia. ERIC, 1972. 41p.

145. Harvey, John F.
(Guidelines for developing a good Engineering School Library at Polytechnic). 1968. (Mimeographed).

146. Harvey, John F.
Indonesian national health science library, documentation center and network plan. New Delhi: World Health Organization, South-East Asia Regional Office, 1979. 64p.

147. Harvey, John F.
(Memorandum on new building planning for the National Library, Teheran). 8 April 1968.

148. Harvey, John F.
Proposal for Pahlavi University Library building consultation. University of Teheran, College of Education, Department of Library Science, 5 February 1968.

149. Harvey, John F.
Report to Chancellor Torab Mehra covering recommendations for the development of Jundi Shapur University library services. University of Teheran, College of Education, Department of Library Science, 1968.

150. Harvey, John F.
Suggestions for organizing a library in the Ministry of Economics Export Development Department.... Tehran: University of Teheran, Department of Library Science, 1968. (Mimeographed).

151. Harvey, John F.
Suggestions for organizing and developing the University of Teheran Institute of Co-operative Research and Studies Library. University of Teheran, College of Education, Department of Library Science, 26 January 1968.

152. Harvey, John F.
Teheran Book Processing Center (TEBROC) proposal draft. University of Teheran, College of Education, Department of Library Science, 2 February 1968.

153. Harvey, John F.
Various memoranda and documents for development of various types of libraries and library services at the University of Teheran. Tehran: University of Teheran, Department of Library Science, 1968. (Mimeographed).

154. Hayes, Francis; Green, Charles B.
Eastern Islands agricultural education (Indonesia). Jakarta: U.S.A.I.D., Bureau for Asia, 16 July 1978. 86p.

A University of Washington team, in conjunction with the U.S.A.I.D. contingency, conducted individual studies of the member universities comprising the Association of Eastern Islands Universities, in order to lay the groundwork for an upcoming project designed to upgrade the curriculum and staff credentials within the universities' agricultural schools.... A familiar litany of weaknesses were identified at each university—lack of textbooks and equipment, inadequate language training, and the need for staff upgrading.

Keywords: Indonesia; agriculture education; agriculture library; university linkage.

DOC. NO. PD-AAF-895-F1.

155. Helal, A.H.
Outline for a national documentation and information centre: United Arab Emirates—(mission) 15 December 1974–2 January 1975. December 1975. 16p., map.

Mission report evaluating the state of library services and information services in the United Arab Emirates—discusses plans by the Union of Arab Broadcasting Organizations for establishing a Gulf Communication Documentation Centre to deal with questions of braodcasting, including educational broadcasting; examines the national information policy and necessary documentation/library co-operation to avoid duplication of resources; provides a section on educational development in the United Arab Emirates, containing educational statistics and enrolment ratios.

UNESCO DOC. CODE: FMR/COM/DND/75/135; RP/1973–74/4.221.1/Technical report. MICROFICHE: 76fr0115. (Restricted).

156. Helal, A.H.
Scientific documentation centre: Iraq—(mission) February–April 1972. August 1972. 64p. (in various pagings), tables, charts.

Mission report on the establishment of a documentation centre for scientific information in Iraq—refers to the need to co-ordinate and reorganize existing facilities, including library services, to set up a union catalogue, to organize inter-library loans, bibliographic services, translation services and reprography; deals with questions of documentation/library personnel and professional training, particularly library training and documentation training; considers plans to introduce computerized documentation at a later stage.

UNESCO DOC. CODE: 2736/RMO.RD/DBA. MICROFICHE: 73fr0021. (Restricted).

157. Hemptinne, Yvan de; Price, D.J. de Solla; Dobrov, Gennady M.; Reheem, K.
Current problems in science and technology policy: Arab Republic of

Egypt—(mission) May 1972. September 1972. 22p. (in various pagings).

Mission report on science policy in Egypt—draws attention to the need for an estimation of technological and scientific potential, especially in human resources; refers to problems of science education and technical training; advises on research policy, transfer of technology, the procurement of scientific instruments and scientific information.

UNESCO DOC. CODE: 2753/RMO.RD/SP. MICROFICHE: 73fr0112. (Restricted).

158. Henkle, H.H.
Pakistan National Science Libraries and Information Centres (July–August 1966) and recruitment and training of personnel (September 1966). November 1966. 23 + 4p.

UNESCO DOC. CODE: WS/1166.114-AVS.

159. Heyman, J.M.
Report on literature search, documentation and related information on Mauritania. 1978. 59p.

Keywords: documentation; information systems; organization; information; information centres; institutions; Mauritania.

U.S.A.I.D. CONTRACT NO. AID/AFR-c-1428. DOC. NO. PN-AAG-941.

160. Heymowski, Adam.
Mauritanie: organisation de la bibliothèque nationale de Mauritanie, Nouakchott (Septembre 1964–février 1965). Paris: Unesco, 1965. 20p., annexes.

UNESCO DOC. CODE: WS/0765.94-CUA/Consultant.

161. Heymowski, Adam.
Organisation de la Bibliothèque nationale de Mauritanie à Nouakchott—(deuxième mission) février–juillet 1971. March 1972. 19p., map.

Mission report dealing with the organization of the national library in Mauritania—covers the compilation of a general bibliography devoted to Mauritania and the updating of a catalogue of Mauritanian manuscripts written in Arabic; also refers to questions of cataloguing and classification.

UNESCO DOC. CODE: 2644/RMO.RD/DBA. MICROFICHE: 73fr0130. (Restricted).

162. Heymowski, Adam.
Renforcement de la Bibliothèque nationale: Mauritanie—(mission). Résultats et recommendations du project. 11 May 1977. 21p. (in various pagings), maps.

Mission report on documentation/library development and documentation/library administration at the national library in Mauritania—describes the organization of the library collection of Arabic manuscripts, and other documentation/library operations such as cataloguing; recommends the in-service training of documentation/library personnel and a more active acquisitions policy.

Keywords: information/library development; information/ library administration; national libraries; Mauritania—library collections; Arabic manuscripts; information/library operations; cataloguing; in-service training; information/library personnel; acquisitions. **Identifiers:** Bibliothèque nationale (Mauritania).

UNESCO DOC. CODE: FMR/PGI/77/225 (UNDP); UNDP/ MAU/74/010/Rapport final. MICROFICHE: 78fr0048. (Restricted).

163. Heyneman, Alan Lionel.
Afghan library development plan . . . prepared for H.E. Dr. Abdul Madjid, Minister of Education. Kabul, 1955. (Typewritten).

164. Hockey, S.W.
Development of public library services: Indonesia—(mission) 28 May–23 June 1976. 2 November 1976. 13p. (in various pagings).

Mission report on documentation/library development in Indonesia, with emphasis on public libraries—discusses the development of the national library service; briefly mentions documentation/library legislation; stresses the importance of developing library training to fill the needs for trained documentation/library personnel.

UNESCO DOC. CODE: FMR/CC/DBA/76/155; RP/1975–76/ 4.221.2/Technical report. MICROFICHE: 77fr0089.

165. Hopkins, Margaret L.
A tentative report on the University of Tehran Library. 1 November 1965. (Mimeographed).

166. Hubert, J.M.
Centre régional de documentation et d'information scientifiques en écologie tropicale: République Unie du Cameroun—(mission) 5–15 août 1978. 31 December 1978. 26p.

Keywords: scientific information systems; documentation centre; ecology; tropical zones; information processing automation; MAB programme; regional co-operation; Cameroon UR—compatibility; international information systems. **Identifiers:** Centre régional de documentation et d'information scientifiques en écologie tropicale (Cameroon UR).

UNESCO DOC. CODE: FMR/SC/ECO/78/168; RP/1977–78/ 2.151.1/Rapport de mission. MICROFICHE: 79fr0136. (Restricted).

167. Hubert, J.M.
Étude des conditions d'implantation à Yaoundé d'un Centre régional de documentation du MAB: République Unie du Cameroun—(mission) 16 janvier–5 février 1978. 1978. 46p., incl. bibl.

Keywords: MAB Programme; scientific information systems; information processing automation; regional co-operation; Cameroon UR—compatibility; international information systems. **Identifiers:** Centre régional de documentation du MAB (Cameroon UR.)

UNESCO DOC. CODE: FMR/SC/ECO/78/114; RP/1977–78/ 2.151.1/Rapport technique. MICROFICHE: 79fr0076. (Restricted).

168. Hunwick, J.O.
Centre de documentation et recherches Ahmad Baba: Mali—(mission) 3–14 février 1974. 5 July 1976. 35p. (in various pagings).

Mission report on a documentation centre and historical research centre in Mali specializing in the collection of manuscripts in Arabic and in African languages dealing with African history—discusses the documentation/library administration and documentation/library personnel of the centre; also examines the various documentation/library operations and services performed, including the conservation of manuscripts; refers to its acquisitions policy and provides the final report of a conference held in 1967 on written source materials for the study of African history.

UNESCO DOC. CODE: FMR/CC/CS/76/122; RP/1975–76/3.311.3/Rapport technique. MICROFICHE: 77fr0111. (Restricted).

169. Ibish, Y.; Al-Ghul, M.
Evaluation of ancient books and manuscripts: Yemen Arab Republic—(mission) September 1971. April 1972. 10p.

Mission report on evaluation of collections of books and manuscripts representative of Moslem ancient civilization and covering the whole range of Arab culture in the Yemen AR—recommends improved pest control, the purchase of library equipment, the setting up of microfilm units and repair workshops and the establishment of library training so as to preserve the cultural heritage.

UNESCO DOC. CODE: 2652/RMO.RD/DBA. MICROFICHE: 72fr0192. (Restricted).

170. Isabel, C.
Regional documentation centre on visual and performing arts: Indonesia—(mission) 13 June–13 July 1976. 31 May 1977. 17p. (in various pagings), illus.

Mission report on the setting up of a research centre on cultural development and a documentation centre for the visual arts and performing arts in Indonesia—describes the functions of the centres and their documentation/library operations based on information user needs; considers the cultural financing and resources required, and refers to documentation/library personnel.

Keywords: research centres; cultural development; documentation centre; visual arts; performing arts; Indonesia—information/library operations; information user needs; cultural financing; information/library personnel.

UNESCO DOC. CODE: FMR/CC/CD/77/160; PP/1975-76/ 3.321.7/Technical report. MICROFICHE: 77fr0144. (Restricted).

171. Islam, S.I.
Abstracting services, National Documentation Centre, Khartoum: Sudan—(mission) 31 October 1980. 8p. (in various pagings).

Keywords: abstracting and indexing services; documentation centres; scientific publications; Sudan—information/library personnel. **Identifiers:** National Documentation Centre (Sudan).

UNESCO DOC. CODE: FMR/PGI/OPS/80/251 (UNDP); UNDP/ SUD/74/036/Assignment report. MICROFICHE: 81fr0014. (Restricted).

172. Itayem, Mahmud A.
ALDOC manpower requirements and development: League of Arab States—(mission) 31 December 1980. 33p., incl. bibl.

Keywords: information science training; information/library personnel; scientific information system; Arab States—training methods; training courses; information/library schools; information/library administration; job description; wages; curriculum development; educational costs. **Identifiers:** Centre for Documentation and Information of the Arab League.

UNESCO DOC. CODE: FMR/PGI/OPS/80/256 (UNDP); UNDP/ RAB/79/030/Assignment report. MICROFICHE: 81fr0036. (Restricted).

173. Jeffreys, A.E.
Arab Republic of Egypt: mechanisation of the catalogues of the National Library, October 1970–April 1971. Paris: Unesco, 1971. 25 + 7 + 22 + 8p.

174. Jeffreys, Alan E.
L'Automatisation des catalogues de la Bibliothèque nationale: Tunisie—(mission) 10 janvier–9 mars 1977. 12 September 1977. 42p., incl. bibl.

Mission report on the introduction of a computerized catalogue at the national library in Tunisia—describes the documentation/library operations and examines possibilities in computer applications for computer-aided compilation of the union catalogue, recommending the ISIS system; discusses computer programming for the national bibliography; also refers to the adaptation of computer software to the Arabic alphabet, and in-service training in computer science education for documentation/library personnel.

Keywords: computerized catalogues; national libraries; Tunisia—information/library operations; computer-assisted compilation; union catalogues; computer programming; national bibliographies; computer software; Arabic; in-service training; computer science education; information/library personnel. **Identifiers:** Bibliothèque nationale (Tunisia). ISIS.

UNESCO DOC. CODE: FMR/BEP/PGI/77/183; RP/1975-76/4.221.2/Rapport technique. MICROFICHE: 78fr0106. (Restricted).

175. Jeffreys, A.E.
Mechanization of the national library catalogues: Egypt—(mission) October–November 1974. March 1975. 23p. (in various pagings), incl. bibl.

Mission report on the development of the computerized catalogue at the national library of Egypt—considers a system of bibliographic control as a component of the automated system; describes the introduction of ISBN and ISBD into the system design; discusses the adaptation of computer software to local needs and the Arabic alphabet; refers to an in-service library training course for library personnel.

UNESCO DOC. CODE: 3158/RMO.RD/DBA. MICROFICHE: 75fr0090.

176. Jones, Graham A.
Science and technology planning: Bangladesh—(mission) 22 June–13 July 1974. February 1975. 42p., illus.

Mission report on science planning in Bangladesh so as to build up its scientific potential—discusses the present science policy and science administration, referring to research councils responsible for scientific research; deals with science education with particular mention of higher technical education and its curriculum development; briefly considers the need to provide

The Bibliography 75

adequate scientific equipment and scientific information for education and industry.

UNESCO DOC. CODE: 3130/RMO.RD/STD. MICROFICHE: 75fr0035. (Restricted).

177. Kabesh, Ahmed Abdel-Hamed.
Development of the Bangladesh National Scientific and Technical Documentation Centre (BANSDOC)—(mission) 28 December 1974–27 January 1975. 1975. 32p. (in various pagings), plan.

Mission report on a national documentation centre dealing with technical and scientific information in Bangladesh—refers to the need for basic data for science policy making; describes the role of documentation services in promoting a research and development programme and the national economic and social development; discusses the documentation/library planning and information policy related to this centre; provides documentation/library statistics, including an estimate of manpower needs for documentation/library personnel.

UNESCO DOC. CODE: FMR/COM/DND/75/139; PP/1973-74/4.221.3/Technical report. MICROFICHE: 76fr0113. (Restricted).

178. Kalia, D.R.
National Library of Iraq: Baghdad—(mission) 28 February 1979. 44p., illus.

Keywords: information/library development; national libraries; Iraq—public libraries; academic libraries; school libraries; special libraries; information/library legislation; information/library administration; library buildings; library equipment; information/library personnel; library training. **Identifiers:** National Library (Iraq).

UNESCO DOC. CODE: FMR/BEP/PGI/79/106; PP/1977-78/5.1.5/Technical report. MICROFICHE: 79fr0188. (Restricted).

179. Kalia, D.R.
Report on a mission to some of the Arab States. Arab States Fundamental Education Centre, 1957.

180. Kamm, Anthony.
Book development: Gambia—(mission) 1–31 March 1976. 15 February 1977. 15p.

Mission report assessing book needs in Gambia and advising on book development, with special emphasis on textbook production—underlines the need for the establishment of an independent publishing organization for book production and the production of other printed teaching materials, especially in vernacular languages; recommends the setting-up of a book rental scheme, tying in book selection with curriculum planning.

Keywords: book needs; Gambia; book development; textbook production—publishing; book production; teaching materials; vernacular languages; book selection; curriculum planning.
UNESCO DOC. CODE: FMR/CC/DBA/77/102; RP/1975–76/4.141.3/End-of-assignment report. MICROFICHE: 77fr0145. (Restricted).

181. Keene, James.; Thomas, D.L.
Conservation of ancient manuscripts: Sultanate of Oman—(mission) 31 May 1980. 27p., illus., plan.

Keywords: manuscripts; cultural heritage; archive records preservation; Oman (Sultanate)—conservation; records management; microfilms; microform equipment; cultural personnel training; cultural costs; damage; glossaries.
UNESCO DOC. CODE: FMR/PGI/80/109; PP/1979–80/5/10.1/05/Technical report. MICROFICHE: 80fr0133. (Restricted).

182. Ketelaar, Eric.
Archival training: Republic of Indonesia—(mission) 31 August 1980. 28p., illus., incl. bibl.

Keywords: archive science training; information/library schools; archive development; archive personnel; Indonesia—national archives; records management; educational planning; curriculum development; university curriculum. **Identifiers:** National Archival Training School (Indonesia).
UNESCO DOC. CODE: FMR/PGI/80/154; RP/1979–80/5/10.1/05/Technical report. MICROFICHE: 81fr0012. (Restricted).

183. Key, L.C.
Report and proposals on the establishment and improvement of libraries and library services in Pakistan. Karachi: 1956. 158p.

184. El-Kheiro, Misbah Muhammad.
Feasibility study on the proposed Arab Regional Centre for Communication Research and Documentation. 1979. 54p., illus., incl. bibl.

Keywords: communication research; documentation centre; information services; feasibility studies; Arab States—information user needs; administrative structure; information sources; information/library personnel; manpower needs. **Identifiers:** Arab Regional Centre for Communication Research and Documentation (proposed). ALECSO Meeting of Experts on Communication Research and Documentation, Cairo, 1978.

UNESCO DOC. CODE: CC.79/WS/28. MICROFICHE: 80S0772.

185. Kirk, Albert.
United Arab Republic: proposed national press for scientific productions, March 1965. Paris: Unesco, 1965.

186. Krentz, Edgar.
Library consultant program report to ATENE: Lebanon and U.A.R. Beirut: 20 November 1968.

187. Kuhlman, A.F.
Turkey: plans for a central general library at the Middle East Technical University. Paris: Unesco, 1964. 33p.

UNESCO DOC. CODE: CUa/TUR/1.

188. Lafont, Suzanne.
La formation et le perfectionnement de spécialistes de l'information documentaire: République populaire du Bénin—(mission) 1 October 1982. 119p.

Keywords: information science training; in-service training; Benin—training courses; curriculum development; national information systems; information/library policy. **Identifiers:** Centre de formation administrative et de perfectionnement (Benin).

UNESCO DOC. CODE: FMR/PGI/82/158; RP/1981–83/5/10.1/05/Rapport technique. MICROFICHE: 83fr0068. (Restricted).

189. Lafont, Suzanne.
Programme de formation en sciences et techniques de l'information de

l'Université nationale: République populaire du Bénin—(mission) 10 August 1983. 18p. (in various pagings), incl. bibl.

Keywords: information science training; document processing; indexing; university curriculum; training courses; university courses; Benin—curriculum development; teaching materials. **Identifiers:** Université nationale (Benin).

UNESCO DOC. CODE: FMR/PGI/83/149; RP/1981-83/5/10.1/05/Rapport de mission. MICROFICHE: 83fr0180. (Restricted).

190. Laiko, V.
United Arab Republic: a mechanized information retrieval system for the Documentation Centre in Cairo, July–September 1968. Paris: Unesco, 1969. 88p.

191. Lajeunesse, Marcel.
Assistance à l'Ecole des sciences de l'information: Maroc—(mission) 19 August 1980. 11p. (in various pagings).

Keywords: information/library schools; information science training; Morocco—curriculum development; university curriculum; university libraries.

UNESCO DOC. CODE: FMR/PGI/OPS/80/246 (UNDP); UNDP/MOR/74/003/Rapport de mission. MICROFICHE: 80fr0160. (Restricted).

192. Lancour, Harold.
Book survey team report on libraries in Iran. [1966?]

193. Lancour, H.
Libraries in British West Africa: a report of a survey for the Carnegie Corporation of New York. October–November 1957. Urbana, Ill.: University of Illinois Library School, 1958. 32p.

194. Lancour, Harold.
Report of survey mission to Mali. January 30, 1963. (Mimeographed).

195. Larsen, Knud.
East Africa: East African School of Librarianship, March 1963–December 1964. Paris: Unesco, 1964. (Mimeographed).

196. Lāzār, Peter.
The information system of the Arab States Broadcasting Union: League of Arab States—(mission) 9 September 1981. 20p.

Keywords: information systems; information services; broadcasting organization; Arab States—data banks; information processing; computerized indexes; information/library personnel; computer hardware; on-line information systems. **Identifiers:** Arab States Broadcasting Union, Information Unit. League of Arab States. Documentation Centre.

UNESCO DOC. CODE: FMR/PGI/OPS/81/260 (UNDP); UNDP/ RAB/79/030/Assignment report. MICROFICHE: 81fr0241. (Restricted).

197. Lāzār, Peter.
The internal system of the Documentation and Information Centre of the Arab League—(mission) 14 September 1981. 38p., incl. bibl.

Keywords: scientific information systems; information/library planning; Arab States—information/library role; information/library administration; administrative structure; information/library personnel; acquisitions; information processing; information services. **Identifiers:** Centre for Documentation and Information of the Arab League.

UNESCO DOC. CODE: FMR/PGI/OPS/81/252 (UNDP); UNDP/ RAB/79/030/Assignment report. MICROFICHE: 82fr0011. (Restricted).

198. Lāzār, Peter.
Outline of the Arab League Information System—(mission) 17 August 1981. 38p.

Keywords: scientific information systems; information services; information/library planning; systems analysis; Arab States—data processing; information/library standards; information science training; information/library personnel; information/library co-operation; information/library administration; administrative structure; information/library budgets. **Identifiers:** League of Arab States, Documentation Centre. Arab League Information Systems.

UNESCO DOC. CODE: FMR/PGI/OPS/81/251 (UNDP); UNDP/

RAB/79/030/Assignment report. MICROFICHE: 82fr0010. (Restricted).

199. Leblanc, Ch.
Création du Centre de documentation et d'études de Carthage: Tunisie—(mission) 4 septembre–4 octobre 1975. 59p., illus., plans.

Mission report on the establishment of a documentation centre and research centre for cultural research at the archaeological site of the ancient city of Carthage, Tunisia—describes in detail the documentation/library planning of the centre and the mehtod of classification to be used to compile catalogues of archaeological objects, historic monuments and the archaeological excavations being carried out; makes suggestions for the development of cultural tourism.

UNESCO DOC. CODE: FMR/SHC/OPS/75/142; PP/1975–76/3.411.6/Rapport technique. MICROFICHE: 76fr0069. (Restricted).

200. Lenz, W.
Mission to Somalia, 30 March–1 April 1976. International Council of Archives, 1976.

201. Lohrer, Alice.
'Library development plans for Gondi Shahpoor University', in *Fulbright Study Team's Report on Gondi Shahpoor University*; development possibilities and priorities. April 1967), p. 57–71.

202. Lombard, E.J.
Liban: évaluation et developpement des bibliothèques (novembre–décembre 1964). Paris: Unesco, 1965. 18p.

203. Maignien, R.
Planification de la recherche écologique: République du Niger—(mission) 25 October 1976.

Mission report on research planning for ecology studies in Niger—outlines the interdisciplinary research being undertaken at present; suggests research co-ordination through the creation of a national committee for the MAB Programme; recommends the drawing up of maps making an ecological analysis of the country, and the establishment of a documentation centre for scientific information.

UNESCO DOC. CODE: FMR/SC/ECO/76/149; RP/1975–76/2.212.5/Rapport technique. MICROFICHE: 76fr0159. (Restricted).

204. Mansour, Joseph M.
Educational and vocational guidance in secondary schools in Kuwait—(mission) 30 November 1982. 62p.

Keywords: educational guidance; vocational guidance; secondary education; Kuwait—educational guidance personnel; educational personnel training; educational testing; educational information; information services; educational projects; project design; project implementation; evaluation of education; project evaluation.

UNESCO DOC. CODE: FMR/ED/OPS/82/278 (UNDP); UNDP/KUW/80/005/Assignment report. MICROFICHE: 83fr0036. (Restricted).

205. Massil, Stephen W.
Study of the feasibility of using MARC tapes for co-operative processing: Malaysia—(mission) 31 August 1977. 57p., incl. bibl.

Mission report presenting a feasibility study for the national library and university libraries in Malaysia on computer applications to documentation/library operations, in this case centralized cataloguing using MARC magnetic tapes; reviews the problems and advantages of information processing automation and of documentation/library co-operation—discusses aspects of the MARC data base and documentation/library financing of the system; provides documentation/library statistics.

Keywords: feasibility studies; national libraries; university libraries; Malaysia; computer applications; information/library operations; centralized cataloguing; magnetic tapes; information processing automation; information/library co-operation—data bases, information/library financing; information/library statistics. **Identifiers:** National Library (Malaysia). MARC System.

UNESCO DOC. CODE: FMR/BEP/PGI/77/190; RP/1975–76/4.221.2/Technical report. MICROFICHE: 78fr0080.

206. Matók, György; Jacsó, Péter.
Identification of training requirements for computerized information services: Iraq—(mission) 6 June 1983. 29p.

Keywords: research councils; documentation centres; information services; information processing automation; training courses; information science training; Iraq—library automation; information retrieval; selective dissemination of information. **Identifiers:** Scientific Research Council (Iraq), Documentation Centre. CDS/ISIS.

UNESCO DOC. CODE: FMR/PGI/OPS/83/236 (UNDP); UNDP/909/ IRQ/84/Assignment report. MICROFICHE: 83fr0093. (Restricted).

207. Mba-Nzé, J.C.
Inventaire du potentiel scientifique et technologique (PST) de la Communauté Afrique—(mission) 19 April 1983. 127p., illus.

Keywords: science and technology; scientific potential; inventories; surveys; West Africa; Ivory Coast; Upper Volta; Mali; Mauritania; Niger; Senegal—intergovernmental organizations; scientific co-operation; science administration; research and development; science policy; policy making; scientific personnel; data collection; data processing; scientific information; scientific institutions; government departments; questionnaires. **Identifiers:** West African Economic Community.

UNESCO DOC. CODE: FMR/SC/STP/83/225 (UNDP); UNDP/RAF/78/067/Rapport de mission. MICROFICHE: 83fr0106. (Restricted).

208. McDonald, Denis; Palmour, Vernon; et al.
Egyptian national system for scientific and technical information: alternatives for library collection development. Rockville, MD.: King Research, Inc., March 1982. 44p.

Keywords: science and technology; information services; libraries; Egypt; reference services; bibliographies; books; abstracts; indexes; periodicals; publishing industry.

U.S. NATIONAL SCIENCE FOUNDATION CONTRACT NO. INT-7924187; PASA NF/EGY-0016-7-77. DOC. NO. PN-AAP-155.

209. McLeroy, George B.
Suggested guidelines for improving the livestock marketing information service of Mali. Washington, D.C.: U.S.A.I.D. Bureau for Technical Assistance, 1974. 21p.

Keywords: livestock; marketing; cattle; information services; Sahel; Mali.

210. Menou, Michel J.
Centre de documentation du Ministère de l'information: Iran—(mission) juin–juillet 1972. August 1972. 60p. (in various pagings), tables.

Mission report on the organization of a documentation centre in Iran with special reference to the study of an information system within the central government, namely the Ministry of Information–describes the functioning of library services, archives and data collection sections; examines cataloguing and classification methods; shows the need for improving the professional library training for documentation/library personnel.

UNESCO DOC. CODE: 2742/RMO.RD/DBA. MICROFICHE: 73fr0016. (Restricted).

211. Menou, Michel J.
Department of Documentation and Information of the Arab League Educational, Cultural and Scientific Organization (ALECSO): Egypt—(mission) 8 November–27 December 1972. May 1973. 23p.

Mission report presenting proposals for information science training for ALECSO's Department of Documentation and Information, Egypt—provides subjects for the curriculum; also makes recommendations concerning the activities of the Department in its field of publishing and considers the functioning of the reprography unit and relevant documentation/library facilities and library equipment.

UNESCO DOC. CODE: 2902/RMO.RD/DBA. MICROFICHE: 73fr0229. (Restricted).

212. Menou, Michel J.
Section des documentalistes, écoles des bibliothécaires, archivistes et documentalistes, de l'Université de Dakar: Sénégal—(mission) fév-

rier–mars 1975. Résultats et recommendations du project. 29 August 1975. 159p. (in various pagings), incl. bibl.

Mission report on documentation training at a documentation/library school in Senegal, giving details on the educational programme of the school and outlining its teaching methods—includes curriculum guides to the courses offered and discusses manpower needs in documentation/library personnel.

UNESCO DOC. CODE: FMR/COM/DND/75/118; RP/PP/1973–74/4.221.3/Rapport final. MICROFICHE: 76fr0035.

213. Montandon, Edmée.
Education concerning the problems associated with the use of drugs: Sierra Leone—(mission) March 1980. 22p. (in various pagings), illus.

Keywords: drug education; drug addiction; seminars; Sierra Leone—dissemination of information; curriculum development; teaching methods; teaching materials; alcoholism. **Identifiers:** Workshop for the Preparation of Educational and Information Material concerning Problems associated with the Use of Drugs, Freetown, 1980.

UNESCO DOC. CODE: FMR/ED/SPO/80/219 (UNFDAC) (Sierra Leone); UNFDAC/AC.50191/Assignment report. MICROFICHE: 80fr0119. (Restricted).

214. Munier, Henri.
Planification de l'éducation et de l'information: Algérie—(mission) janvier 1969–octobre 1971. March 1972. 10p.

Mission report on educational planning in Algeria—emphasizes the need for recruitment and educational personnel training, including those responsible for the planning of human resources development; recommends an improved information system and the setting up of a computer centre, with a view to making wider use of the computer facilities available.

UNESCO DOC. CODE: 2640/RMO.RD/EP; RM/AT/ALGERED 15. MICROFICHE: 73fr0110. (Restricted).

215. Munn, Robert.
The University of Gezira Library: a planning report. Khartoum: Ford Foundation, 1977.

216. Munroe, Jean F.
Development of marine science libraries in Indonesia—(mission) 31 October 1979. 55p., incl. bibl.

Keywords: information/library development; scientific libraries; oceanography; Indonesia—information/library facilities; information/library resources; library training; information/library administration; information/library budgets; library collections; acquisition policy; information/library personnel.
Identifiers: National Institute of Oceanology Library (Indonesia).

UNESCO DOC. CODE: FMR/PGI/OPS/79/249 (UNDP); UNDP/INS/74/029/Assignment report. MICROFICHE: 79fr0224. (Restricted).

217. Myatt, A.
Scientific and technical information services: Indonesia—(mission) July 1973. 128p., tables, incl. bibl.

Mission report describing the development in Indonesia of a network of special libraries, research libraries and documentation centres for science and technology, including agriculture and biology—examines the structure and functions of the present information services for scientific information; stresses the need for professional library training.

UNESCO DOC. CODE: 2931/RMO.RD/SP; FR/UNDP/Consultant. MICROFICHE: 73fr0262. (Restricted).

218. Al-Najdawi, Amin A.M.
Collection building: League of Arab States—(mission) 31 December 1980. 23p., illus.

Keywords: library collections; information sources; acquisition policy; Arab States—information user needs; book selection; periodical acquisition systems; information/library budgets.
Identifiers: Centre for Documentation and Information of the Arab League.

UNESCO DOC. CODE: FMR/PGI/OPS/80/258 (UNDP); UNDP/RAB/79/030/Assignment report. MICROFICHE: 81fr0094. (Restricted).

219. National Documentation Centre: Sudan—(mission). *Project findings and recommendations.* 8 November 1978. 18p.

Keywords: documentation centre; information/library development; information services; library services; national information systems; scientific information systems; Sudan—science policy. **Identifiers:** National Documentation Centre (Sudan).

UNESCO DOC. CODE: FMR/PGI/78/255 (UNDP); UNDP/ SUD-/74/036/Terminal report. MICROFICHE: 79fr0118.

220. *National library system*: Somalia—(mission). *Project findings and recommendations.* 21 December 1977. 59p. (in various pagings), incl. bibl.

Mission report on documentation/library planning and documentation/library legislation for the proposed national library in Somalia—discusses the co-ordination of existing library services and the building up of a basic reference service; deals with the need for library training; includes guidelines for the implementation of a national library plan and a national information system.

Keywords: information/library planning; information/library legislation; national libraries; Somalia—library services; reference services; library training; national information systems. **Identifiers:** National Library (Somalia) (proposed).

UNESCO DOC. CODE: FMR/PGI/77/274 (UNDP); UNDP/ SOM/75/013/Terminal report. MICROFICHE: 78fr0095. (Restricted).

221. Navarro Gomez, Lucia.
Centre de documentation, d'études et de recherches en matière culturelle: République de Guinée-Bissau—(mission) 30 June 1979. 35p., illus.

Keywords: cultural research; research centres; documentation centre; Guinea-Bissau—cultural identity; cultural development; cultural resources; cultural personnel; cultural facilities; cultural financing; cultural legislation; cultural planning and administration. **Identifiers:** Centre de documentation, d'études et de recherches en matière culturelle (Guinea-Bissau).

UNESCO DOC. CODE: FMR/CC/CD/79/163; PP/1977–78/ 4.131.5/Rapport technique. MICROFICHE: 80fr0037. (Restricted).

222. N'Diaye, A.G.
Organisation commune Africaine, Malagache et Mauricienne: reorganisation du service de documentation, archives et bibliothèque (suite), avril–mai 1974. Paris: Unesco, 1974. 7p.

UNESCO DOC. CODE: 3095/RMO.RD/DBA.

223. Negus, A.E.
Development of the Scientific Documentation Centre: Iraq—(mission) 15 April 1983. 12p.

Keywords: documentation centres; scientific information; information/library development; Iraq. **Identifiers:** Council of Scientific Research (Iraq), Scientific Documentation Centre.

UNESCO DOC. CODE: FMR/PGI/83/116; RP/1981–83/5/10.1/ 03/Assignment report. MICROFICHE: 83fr0091. (Restricted).

224. Negus, A.E.
Specification for a feasibility study for the establishment of an Arab data network for information interchange: Federation of Arab Scientific Research Councils—(mission) 30 May 1983. 5p.

Keywords: scientific information systems; information exchange; feasibility studies; Arab countries. **Identifiers:** Federation of Arab Scientific Research Councils. Arab Scientific and Technological Information Network (proposed).

UNESCO DOC. CODE: FMR/PGI/83/126; RP/1981–83/5/10.1/ 03/Assignment report. MICROFICHE: 83fr0099. (Restricted).

225. *Network of scientific information and documentation*: Indonesia—(mission). Project findings and recommendations. 12 December 1980. 43p. (in various pagings).

Keywords: information/library networks; scientific information systems; information services; information/library co-operation; Indonesia—documentation centres; information exchange; information user needs; information processing; reference services; document storage; oceanography; human settlement; library collections; abstracting and indexing services; current awareness services; data processing; telecommunication; information science training; information/library personnel. **Identifiers:** National Scientific and Technological Documentation Centre (Indonesia). National Institute of Oceanology Library (Indonesia). Hasanuddin University Library (Indonesia). Human Settlements Information System (Indonesia).

UNESCO DOC. CODE: FMR/PGI/OPS/80/267 (UNDP); UNDP/INS/74/029/Terminal report. MICROFICHE: 81fr0053. (Restricted).

226. Nugue, Charles.
Formation artistique et formation des personnels de l'action culturelle; maisons de la culture: Algérie—(mission) 31 May 1980. 90p.

Keywords: cultural centres; cultural personnel training; art education; cultural action; animation culturelle; Algeria—cultural policy; cultural legislation; curriculum development; university curriculum; music education; plastic arts; performing arts; cultural agents training; evaluation of education; cultural activities; cultural equipment; libraries; cultural administration. **Identifiers:** Algeria, Ministère de l'information et de la culture.

UNESCO DOC. CODE: FMR/CC/CD/80/119; RP/PP/1977-78/4.131.5/Rapport technique. MICROFICHE: 80fr0161. (Restricted).

227. Olier, J.H.d'.
La création du réseau national de l'information scientifique et technique du Sénégal—(mission) 19 May 1981. 47p., illus.

Keywords: national information systems; information services; information/library networks; information/library planning; Senegal—information user instruction; information/library centralization; document processing; information/library cooperation. **Identifiers:** Réseau national de l'information scientifique et technique (Senegal).

UNESCO DOC. CODE: FMR/PGI/OPS/81/233 (UNDP); UNDP/SEN/77/016/Rapport de mission. MICROFICHE: 81fr0171. (Restricted).

228. Olier, J.H.d'.
Création d'un système régional d'échanges d'information à caractère scien-

tifique et partique dans le domaine des ressources en eau: Algérie, Maroc et Tunisie—(mission) 18 March 1982. 40p.

Keywords: water resources management; regional information networks; scientific information; information exchange; Algeria; Morocco; Tunisia—information/library resources; documentation centres; information/library personnel; library services; information services.

UNESCO DOC. CODE: FMR/PGI/OPS/82/213 (UNDP); UNDP/RAB/80/011/Rapport de mission. MICROFICHE: 83fr0076. (Restricted).

229. Orléans, Jacques d'.
Centre régional de formation d'archivistes, Dakar: Sénégal—(mission) 1er janvier 1972–1er août 1973. August 1973. 46p., tables, incl. bibl.

Mission report on regional co-operation in Africa for the establishment of a centre for archive science training, attached to the Ecole des bibliothécaires, archivistes et documentalistes in Senegal—discusses questions of recruitment, fellowships and curriculum development on a level of higher education, with special mention of the study of African cultures; examines the relation of archive education and employment in African countries, describes the various examinations given and refers to missions to Zaire, Rwanda, Burundi, the Ivory Coast and Niger.

UNESCO DOC. CODE: 2953/RMO.RD/DBA; RM/AFRIDOC/SENEGAL 2. MICROFICHE: 74fr0007. (Restricted).

230. Ormanni, Enrica.
Preservation of materials at the National Library, Cairo—(mission) 24 November–8 December 1974. March 1975. 13p. (in various pagings), illus.

Mission report presenting a plan on book preservation at the National Library in Egypt; describes the organization of laboratory services to provide conservation techniques for archive documents, books and bindings.

UNESCO DOC. CODE: 3154/RMO.RD/DBA. MICROFICHE: 76fr0074. (Restricted).

231. Ozinian, Vartan H.G.
Assistance préparatoire a l'Institut national d'études et de recherches du bâtiment: Algérie—(mission) 25 September 1978. 4v.

Keywords: construction engineering; town planning; research centres; administrative structure; Algeria—building materials; building standards; construction industry; architecture; housing; social factors; legislation; professional training; professional personnel; technical personnel; information services. **Identifiers:** Institut national d'études et de recherches du bâtiment (Algeria).

UNESCO DOC. CODE: FMR/SC/OPS/78/249 (UNDP); UNDP/ALG/77/046/Rapport de mission. MICROFICHE: 79fr0117. (Restricted).

232. Palmer, R.P.; Mahmoud, U.E.; Albin, M.W.
Department of Librarianship and Archival Studies and University of Cairo libraries; fact resource paper and evaluation and recommendations. Cairo: U.S. Agency for International Development, Bureau for Near East, 1978. 90p.

Keywords: libraries; library science education; evaluation; universities; Egypt.

DOC. NO. PN-AAG-438.

233. Palmer, R.P.; Mahmoud, U.E.
University of Minia co-ordinated libraries and user services and library education programs; a planning report. Cairo: U.S. Agency for International Development, Bureau for Near East, 1978. 43p.

Keywords: libraries; library science education; universities; Egypt.

DOC. NO. PN-AAG-439.

234. Pansini, Giuseppe.
Réorganisation des archives nationales: Gabon—(mission) novembre–décembre 1972. September 1973. 33p. (in various pagings).

Mission report describing the reorganization of the national archives in Gabon—refers to collection of all materials concerning the central government; mentions the recruitment and archive science training of the staff.

UNESCO DOC. CODE: 2965/RMO.RD/DBA. MICROFICHE: 74fr0021. (Restricted).

235. Parker, Stephen J.
Arab Gulf States Folklore Centre; establishment of an information centre: Qatar—(mission) 26 January 1984. 44p.

Keywords: folklore; cultural centres; information services; data bases; information/library development; cultural information; Arab culture; Gulf States; Qatar—information user needs; information/library operations; library services; library buildings; library equipment; information/library personnel. **Identifiers:** Arab Gulf States Folklore Centre (Qatar), Information Centre.

UNESCO DOC. CODE: FMR/PGI/OPS/84/201/Technical report. MICROFICHE: 84fr0050. (Restricted).

236. Parker, Stephen J.
Bangladesh public library survey: final report. Bath: Library Development Consultants, 1979. 3 vols.

237. Parker, Stephen J.
Development of a school and public libraries network: Kuwait—(mission) 1–31 December 1974. 25 August 1975. 85p.

Mission report on documentation/library development in Kuwait, with emphasis on school libraries and public libraries—includes a brief country report and a discussion on the estimated potential user population; describes information user needs and the library collections of various libraries, with reference to their relation to book production and supply; also considers documentation/library administration and documentation/library operations; deals with library services, making mention of differences among libraries in the country; lists proposals for library development under a five-year plan of 1975–80, with special reference to documentation/library personnel; provides documentation/library statistics.

UNESCO DOC. CODE: FMR/COM/DND/75/115; PP/1973–74/4.211.2/Technical report. MICROFICHE: 76fr0003.

238. Parker, Stephen J.
Development of documentation, library and archives services: Libyan Arab Republic—(mission) 2–30 May 1976. 15 November 1976. 128p., illus.

Mission report on the evaluation of documentation/library planning for documentation/library development and archive development in the Libyan AR—discusses preconditions of library development, referring briefly to potential information users and book production; examines the country's documentation/library legislation and the organization of its documentation/library administration; studies all types of libraries and information services, such as public libraries, school libraries, and cultural centres; also covers university libraries, special libraries and national archives; reports on documentation/library personnel for performing documentation/library operations in these various types of libraries and documentation centres; concludes with a section on policy for a national information system within the NATIS programme; provides general statistical data for the country, as well as documentation/library statistics.

UNESCO DOC. CODE: FMR/CC/DBA/76/152; PP/1975–76/4.211.3/Technical report. MICROFICHE: 77fr0090.

239. Parker, Stephen J.; Sewell, Philip Hooper.
Development of library and documentation services: Democratic Republic of the Sudan—(mission) March 1972. July 1972. 94p., tables, charts, maps, incl. bibl.

Mission report presenting a survey on the trends of development of library services and information services and their role in educational development in the Democratic Republic of the Sudan—urges the elaboration of legislation regulating the relationship between education and communication; details the proposed plan of action which covers recruitment and professional education in library science, communication research and book production; includes statistical data on school libraries and public libraries.

UNESCO DOC. CODE: 2728/RMO.RD/DBA. MICROFICHE: 73fr0144. (Restricted).

240. Parker, Stephen J.
'Proposals for library development in the Hashemite Kingdom of Jordan', *Rissalat al-maktaba* 10(4), 11–15, 1975

241. Pearce, Douglas E.
Book development: Indonesia—(mission) September–December 1973. June 1974. 90p., illus.

Mission report examining book development in Indonesia, especially the problems connected with book production, publishing and book distribution and their solution within the framework of a five year development plan—considers textbook production for primary education, secondary education and higher education, as well as reading materials for new literates; recommends the creation of a national book development council to consolidate the book industry and better serve the book needs of the country.

UNESCO DOC. CODE: FMR/PGI/79/134; RP/1977-78/5.13.4/72/024. MICROFICHE: 74fr0148. (Restricted).

242. Pelou, Pierre.
L'Organisation micrographique des dossiers au Centre de documentation nationale, Tunis: Tunisie—(mission) 31 May 1979. 21p., illus.

Keywords: microforms; file organization; file maintenance; documentation centre; Tunisia—microfiche; microfilms; microform equipment; information/library personnel; information/library budgets; information/library administration. **Identifiers:** Centre de documentation nationale (Tunisia).

UNESCO DOC. CODE: FMR/PGI/79/134; RP/1977-78/5.13.4/ Rapport technique. MICROFICHE: 79fr0203. (Restricted).

243. Pérotin, Y.
Algérie: archives publiques (avril–juillet 1964). Paris: Unesco, 1964. 61p.

244. Pérotin, Y.
Irak: organisation des archives, février–avril 1970. Paris: Unesco 1970.

245. Pérotin, Y.
Maroc: préservation et classification des archives, novembre 1968–février 1969. Paris: Unesco, 1968. 33p.

246. Pfetsch, Frank R.
Information base for national R and D planning: Indonesia—(mission) July 1973. 33p., charts, diagrs., table, incl. bibl.

Mission report concerning the development of an information system within the framework of the Institute of Sciences of

Indonesia to be used for national research and development planning in science and technology—outlines the administrative framework responsible for research co-ordination and data collection; examines questions of scientific financing; refers to a study of scientific potential including human resources for development planning; recommends close collaboration with the National Development Planning Agency.

UNESCO DOC. CODE: 2939/RMO.RD/SP; FR/UNDP/Consultant. MICROFICHE: 73fr0266. (Restricted).

247. Pfetsch, Frank R.
Science, technology and development; Iraq—(mission) 27 August–13 October 1975. 16 March 1976. 46p. (in various pagings), illus.

Mission report on science policy and science planning in Iraq, with special reference to the Foundation of Scientific Research and its dissemination of scientific information on scientific potential—describes a documentation centre and information user needs for science information; considers key indicators for national planning, including scientific personnel, technical personnel and scientific expenditures for research and development; recommends the establishment of a national information system for dealing with the national scientific and technical potential; provides science statistics and educational statistics, including enrolment ratios.

UNESCO DOC. CODE: FMR/SC/STP/75/245 (Funds-in-Trust)/ Technical report 1. MICROFICHE: 76fr0091. (Restricted).

248. Piet, David L.
Egypt phase II of a project concerned with population information, education and communication. Washington, D.C.: American Public Health Association, 1978. 61p.

Keywords: family planning; population growth; information services; communications; training facilities; project analysis; project design; family planning education; Egypt.

U.S.A.I.D. CONTRACT NO. AID/PHA-c-1100.

249. Piganiol, Pierre.
Le Centre de planification de la recherche scientifique et technique: Sénégal—(mission) janvier 1972. April 1972. 12p.

Report evaluating the progress of a mission on research planning in science and technology in Senegal—mentions problems of information science; draws attention to economic planning peculiar to developing countries and the need to study each new situation in the light of systems analysis; outlines work remaining to be done in the fields of technical and industrial research and points to the desirability of follow-up of the pilot project.

UNESCO DOC. CODE: 2653/RMO.RD/SP. MICROFICHE: 72fr0219. (Restricted).

250. Piganiol, Pierre.
Planification scientifique et technologique—institutions et méthods: Sénégal—(mission) 1–11 mai 1977. 4 November 1977. 26p.

Mission report presenting an evaluation of science planning in scientific research and science budgeting in Senegal—reviews the roles of various scientific institutions and scientific programmes in carrying out the country's science policy; deals with computer software and the data bank for scientific information and examines the question of standardization.

Keywords: evaluation; science planning; scientific research; science budgets; Senegal—scientific institutions; scientific programmes; science policy; computer software; data banks; scientific information; standardization.

UNESCO DOC. CODE: FMR/SC/STP/77/263 (UNDP); UNDP/SEN/74/003/Rapport technique. MICROFICHE: 78fr0128. (Restricted).

251. Planning and Development Collaborative International, Inc., Washington, D.C.; Sherif El-Hakim and Associates, Cairo.
National urban policy study information system; system manual and general guidelines for integration into broader information systems. Washington, D.C.: Planning and Development Collaborative International, 1982. iii, 19p. + 3 appendices.

Keywords: Egypt; information systems; urban planning—information retrieval; information services; libraries; data storage; manuals.

DOC. NO. PN-AAL-654.

252. Poindron, Paul.
Propositions pour le développement de l'infrastructure des bibliothèques: Tunisie—(mission) août–septembre 1974. May 1975. 21p.

Mission report on documentation/library development in Tunisia—deals with questions concerning the national library, university libraries, special libraries, public libraries and school libraries; also describes related problems of book production and book distribution; refers briefly to documentation/library co-operation and library training.

UNESCO DOC. CODE: 3177/RMO.RD/DBA. MICROFICHE: 75fr0125.

253. Polinière, J.P.
Situation and needs of national information systems in science and technology: East Africa—(mission) 29 October–20 December 1974. October 1975. 77p. (in various pagings), incl. bibl.

Mission report containing a survey of needs in national information systems in six East African Member States: Burundi, Kenya, Rwanda, Tanzania UR, Uganda and Zambia—provides information system evaluation; estimates information user needs in the fields of agriculture and industry; considers problems of regional co-operation in this field.

UNESCO DOC. CODE: FMR/SC/STI/75/132/E; RP/1973–74/2.13.6/Technical report. MICROFICHE: 76fr0038. (Restricted).

254. Pray, Carl E.; Cardwell, Vernon B.; et al.
Agricultural research system of Pakistan: the report of the Minnesota Reconnaissance Team. Minneapolis, MN.: University of Minnesota, Economic Development Center, October 1982. 71p.

Keywords: agricultural research; institutional framework; Pakistan—research facilities; manpower needs; universities; graduate study; libraries; linkages; projects; national planning.

U.S.A.I.D. CONTRACT NO. AID/ASIA-c-1456. DOC. NO. PN-AAM-351.

255. Rajagopalan, T.S.
Development of services in the National Library: Somalia—(mission) 14 June 1983. 10p.

Keywords: library services; information/library development;

national libraries; Somalia–library collections; information/ library personnel. **Identifiers:** National Library of Somalia.

UNESCO DOC. CODE: FMR/PGI/83/136; PP/1981–83/5/10.1/05/Technical report. MICROFICHE: 83fr0158. (Restricted).

256. Rajagopalan, T.S.
Documentation Centre of the Ministry of Foreign Affairs: Sudan—(mission) June 1972–March 1973. July 1973. 46p. (in various pagings), incl. bibl.

Mission report on the establishment of a documentation centre in the Ministry of Foreign Affairs in Sudan to cover the fields of international relations, cultural relations and economic information for the central government personnel—examines the future integration of its present library with the documentation centre and examines all documentation/library operations; considers all phases of documentation and particular reference to information service and selective dissemination of information; briefly refers to its printing and reprography programmes.

UNESCO DOC. CODE: 2942/RMO.RD/DBA; FR/UNDP/Consultant. MICROFICHE: 74fr0018. (Restricted).

257. Ray, David T.
Final report of the School Library Advisor on work with National Pedagogical Institute, Ministry of National Education, Bamako, Mali, 1966–68. June 1968.

258. Redmond, Donald A.
Report on the Library, Middle East Technical University, Ankara, Turkey, July 1959 to June 1960, submitted to Unesco and Middle East Technical University. 1960. 18p.

259. Reicher, Daniel.
Les bibliothèques universitaires: Algérie—(mission) 31 July 1980. 16p.

Keywords: university libraries; information/library planning; Algeria—information/library personnel; information science training; library equipment; information/library resources; acquisition policy; bibliographic services.

UNESCO DOC. CODE: FMR/PGI/80/138; RP/PP/1979–80/5/

98 The Bibliography

10.1/05/Rapport technique. MICROFICHE: 80fr0173. (Restricted).

260. Reicher, Daniel; Balquière, Henri.
Deuxième cycle d'études a l'École de bibliothécaires, archivistes et documentalistes de l'Université de Dakar (EBAD): La République du Sénégal—(mission) 22 July 1981. 29p. (in various pagings).

Keywords: information/library schools; information science training; educational programmes; curriculum planning; Senegal—curriculum development; educational projects; archive science training; information/library personnel; manpower needs; admission criteria. **Identifiers:** Université de Dakar. École de bibliothécaires, archivistes et documentalistes.

UNESCO DOC. CODE: FMR/PGI/81/163; RP/1979–80/5/10/1/05/Rapport technique. MICROFICHE: 81fr0178. (Restricted).

261. Roberts, Kenneth H.
Bibliothèque Nationale, Bénin: rapport d'une mission..., 15–19 juillet, 1976. Paris: Unesco, 1976. 13p.

UNESCO DOC. CODE: CC/DBA.14.

262. Roberts, Kenneth H.; Tocatlian, Jacques.
Co-opération régionale pour la formation des spécialistes de l'information au Maghreb: vers l'établissement d'une école régionale: Maroc, Algérie et Tunisie—(mission) 14–21 juin 1974. 17 July 1974. 15p.

Mission report on regional co-operation in the Maghreb for the establishment of a reigonal documentation/library school in Tunisia for information specialists—describes the documentation training and library training programmes and discusses the different problems of Morocco, Algeria and Tunisia, examines such questions as the language of instruction, admission criteria and equivalence between diplomas.

UNESCO DOC. CODE: 1987/DBA/STD/18/VII/74. MICROFICHE: 75S0355. (Restricted).

263. Roberts, Kenneth H.
Propositions pour le développement des services de bibliothèques et de documentation en Haute-Volta—(mission) 8–17 mars 1976. 29 March 1976. 17p. (in various pagings).

Mission report dealing with documentation/library development in Upper Volta, with special reference to the establishment of a national library—discusses existing documentation/library facilities and the need to improve library services and information services, with particular mention of public libraries; examines documentation/library legislation for strengthening the university libraries, namely that of the Université de Ouagadougou; refers to the collaboration of Saudi Arabia in this university project.

UNESCO DOC. CODE: COM/DND/14. MICROFICHE: 77S0363.

264. Robertson, E.I.
Science and technology policy: Jordan—(mission) 15 July 1983. 22p., incl. bibl.

Keywords: science and technology; science policy; policy making; Jordan—science planning; science administration; government departments; science budgets; research and development; research priorities; scientific information systems; scientific personnel; manpower needs.

UNESCO DOC. CODE: FMR/SC/STP/83/143; RP/1981-83/2/4.2/01/Technical report. MICROFICHE: 83fr0184. (Restricted).

265. Röhr, H.
Somalia: library development (mission) 1963. Unesco, 1965. 5p.

266. Romerio, G.F.
Centre national de documentation; rapport préliminaire sur le project de mécanisation des procédés de recherche documentaire (1971–75): Maroc—(mission) 3 mars–20 avril 1974. 1974. 20p. (in various pagings), illus., incl. bibl.

Mission report on the National documentation centre of Morocco—discusses such questions concerned with the introduction of computerized documentation as information processing, terminology, use of the kwic index and the necessity for a thesaurus; describes content analysis of documents, particularly for scientific information; deals with participation in an information network of international and national archives; refers to information science training and a computer terminal.

UNESCO DOC. CODE: MOR/71/538. MICROFICHE: 74fr0109. (Restricted).

267. Romerio, G.F.
Possibility of an Arab League Information System: League of Arab States—(mission) 10 February 1984. 63p., illus., incl. bibl.

Keywords: scientific information systems; social science information; information/library planning; systems analysis; feasibility studies; Arab countries—computer hardware; computer software; format; information processing; data transmission; teleprocessing; telecommunication links; on-line systems; communication networks. **Identifiers:** League of Arab States, Documentation Centre. ALIS: Arab League Information System.

UNESCO DOC. CODE: FMR/PGI/OPS/84/203 (UNDP); UNDP/RAB/79/030/Assignment report. MICROFICHE: 84fr0052. (Restricted).

268. Romerio, G.F.
A regional centre for scientific and technological information transfer: Iran—(mission) September 1977. 31 December 1977. 31p., incl. bibl.

Mission report presenting a feasibility study on the establishment of a national information system for the information transfer of scientific information in Iran (ISTIS)—examines Iranian information policy and considers the integration of a regional documentation centre for scientific information within the ten-year national library project; discusses options and objectives of the proposed Iranian Scientific and Technological Information System (ISTIS) and recommends, within the framework of the MACRONET principle (UNISIST), the connection to other on-line information systems in order to enlarge the subject coverage of the data bases.

Keywords: feasibility studies; national information systems; information transfer; scientific information systems; Iran—information/library policy; documentation centre; national libraries; on-line information systems; data bases. **Identifiers:** UNISIST.

UNESCO DOC. CODE: FMR/BEP/PGI/77/306; RP/1977–78/5.1.3/Technical report. MICROFICHE: 78fr0153. (Restricted).

269. Romerio, G.F.
A teledocumentation system for the National Information and Documenta-

tion Centre: Arab Republic of Egypt—(mission) 3–30 April 1977. June 1977. 40p., map, incl. bibl.

Mission report on documentation/library development of the National Information and Documentation Centre (NIDOC) through its connection to an international information network, and its role in a national information system in Egypt—describes the centre's library collection and information services; proposes an implementation of NIDOC's documentation/library administration together with suggestions for the creation of an information storage and information retrieval department responsible for all documentary analysis and literature search activities as well as for the technical documentation/library operations of the centre; examines the possibility of the installation of a computer terminal connected to the ESRIN/SDS data bases of the European Space Agency which operate an on-line management system, the need for a microfiche bank, and adoption of the international ASV-CODAR system for data processing activities in Arabic.

Keywords: information/library development; Documentation Centre; information/library networks; national information systems; Egypt—library collections; information services; information/library administration; information processing; information retrieval; documentary analysis; literature searches; information/library operations; computer terminals; data bases; on-line information systems; information/library management; microfiche; data processing; Arabic. **Identifiers:** National Information and Documentation Centre (Egypt). European Space Agency.

UNESCO DOC. CODE: FMR/PGI/77/162 (PROV); RP/1977–78/ Technical report. MICROFICHE: 78fr0015. (Restricted).

270. Romerio, G.F.
A teledocumentation system for the National Information and Documentation Centre: Arab Republic of Egypt—(mission) 3–30 April 1977. 30 September 1977. 35p., incl. bibl.

Mission report on the design of a natioal information system for Egypt based on the National Information and Documentation Centre (NIDOC) specializing in scientific information—describes the present documentation/library facilities and library services provided by the Centre; suggests the creation of

102 The Bibliography

an Information Storage and Information Retrieval Department responsible for information processing and searching activities; proposes within the framework of the MACRONET principle (UNISIST), the installation of a video display computer terminal to be connected to international on-line information systems such as ESRIN/SOS data bases of the European Space Agency.

Keywords: national information systems; Egypt; Documentation Centre; scientific information systems—information/library facilities; library services; information processing; Information Retrieval; searching; computer terminals; on-line information systems; data bases. **Identifiers:** National Information and Documentation Centre (Egypt). UNISIST.

UNESCO DOC. CODE: FMR/PGI/77/162; RP/1977–78/4.13.8/ Technical report. MICROFICHE: 78fr0132. (Restricted).

271. Roper, Michael.
Establishment of a technical training centre in archival restoration and reprography: Democratic Republic of the Sudan—(mission) 31 August 1980. 31p., plans, incl. bibl.

Keywords: archive records preservation; reprography; technical training; training centres; Sudan—curriculum development; educational facilities; educational expenditure. **Identifiers:** Training Centre for Archival Technicians (Sudan).

UNESCO DOC. CODE: FMR/PGI/80/160; RP/1979–80/5/10.1/ 03/Technical report. MICROFICHE: 81fr0011. (Restricted).

272. Rothe, Marshal D.; Larson, Douglas.
Report on the Egyptian state information service's mass media campaign to support population and family planning. Washington, D.C.: American Public Health Association, 1981, 55p.

Keywords: Egypt; family planning; family planning education; mass media; mass communication; information services.

U.S.A.I.D. CONTRACT NO. AID/DSPE-c-0053. DOC. NO. PN-AAJ-483.

273. Rousseau, Henri.
Activités reprographiques du Centre national de documentation scientifique et technique: Sénégal—(mission) 21 May 1980. 7p.

Keywords: reprography; documentation centres; Senegal—

technical personnel; printing equipment; photographic equipment. **Identifiers:** Centre national de documentation scientifique et technique (Senegal).

UNESCO DOC. CODE: FMR/PGI/OPS/80/224 (UNDP); UNDP/ SEN/77/016/Rapport de mission. MICROFICHE: 80fr0126. (Restricted).

274. Rózsa, György.
Development project for the National Library: the Republic of Maldives—(mission) 31 December 1982. 17p.

Keywords: national libraries; information/library development; Maldives—library collections; information/library personnel; information/library legislation. **Identifiers:** National Library (Maldives).

UNESCO DOC. CODE: FMR/PGI/82/179; PP/1981–83/5/10.1/ 05/Technical report. MICROFICHE: 83fr0053. (Restricted).

275. Saith, S.S.
East African School of Librarianship: Uganda—(mission) July 1968–November 1972. 1973. 79p. (in various pagings), tables, incl. bibl.

Mission report dealing with a project of regional co-operation for library training in East Africa—describes the establishment and activities of the East African documentation/library school, with mention of its organizational problems; refers to curriculum development and training courses leading to various diplomas and certificates; examines admission criteria and mentions future projects for training of personnel for special libraries and information services; provides some educational statistics.

UNESCO DOC. CODE: 2924/RMO.RD/DBA; FR/UNDP/Uganda 1. MICROFICHE: 73fr0278. (Restricted).

276. Salah, Munthir.
Computerization of ALDOC activities: League of Arab States—(mission) 7 September 1981. 29p., illus., plan.

Keywords: computer applications; documentation centres; computer programming; Arab States—management information systems; job description; Tunisia. **Identifiers:** League of

Arag States, Documentation Centre. International Development Research Centre (Canada). MINISIS.

UNESCO DOC. CODE: FMR/PGI/OPS/81/258 (UNDP); UNDP/RAB/79/030/Assignment report. MICROFICHE: 81fr0243. (Restricted).

277. Saleeb, Shafeek I.
Establishment of a National Computer Centre: Democratic Republic of Sudan—(mission) 30 November 1980. 30p., map.

Keywords: information services; national information systems; data processing; computer science education; Sudan—computer hardware; computer applications; administrative structure; information/library financing. **Identifiers:** National Computer Centre (Sudan).

UNESCO DOC. CODE: FMR/SC/SER/80/185; RP/1979-80/2/4/3/08/Technical report. MICROFICHE: 81fr0064. (Restricted).

278. Salmona, Jean; Salomonsson, Owe.
Natural resources information system: Indonesia—(mission) July 1973. 41p., fold. chart, tables, incl. bibl.

Mission report concerning information systems on natural resources in Indonesia—examines questions of data collection, information processing and information retrieval and brings out the advantages of computerized documentation.

UNESCO DOC. CODE: 2926/RMO.RD/SP; FR/UNDP/Consultant. MICROFICHE: 73fr0263. (Restricted).

279. Saracevic, Tefko.
East African School of Librarianship; a course in documentation and recommendations for curriculum: Uganda—(mission) 7 August–6 September 1975. 25 May 1976. 33p., incl. bibl.

Mission report describing a university course in documentation training at an East African documentation/library school for students and librarians from Uganda, Kenya and Tanzania UR at Makerere University as part of its programme of library training—analyses the theme of the course as the role of information science in national development, particularly in developing countries; discusses information systems and information services within the NATIS Programme; considers overall educational trends in information science training, as well as regional needs and the current university curriculum of the East African School of Librarianship; proposes changes in the degree structure at the EASL as part of the change in documentation/library development.

UNESCO DOC. CODE: FMR/CC/DBA/76/121; RP/1975–76/ 4.221.3/Technical report. MICROFICHE: 77fr0099. (Restricted).

280. Sarasohn, Homer M.
Information needs and uses in Egypt. Atlanta, Ga.: Georgia Institute of Technology, School of Information and Computer Science, August 1981. iii, 70p.

Keywords: science and technology; information systems; information services; Egypt; socioeconomic development; communications management; communications technology; systems analysis; professional personnel.

U.S. NATIONAL SCIENCE FOUNDATION CONTRACT NO. INT-7924187; PASA NF/EGY-0016-7-77. DOC. NO. PN-AAP-074.

281. Sauçois, Christiane.
Création d'un service de restauration et de reprographic à la Bibliothèque centrale universitaire d'Istanbul: Turquie—(mission) 24 octobre–23 novembre 1976. 31 December 1976. 10p. (in various pagings).

Mission report on the establishment of a restoration and reprography service in one of the university libraries in Turkey for the purpose of manuscript and book preservation—briefly describes the rare books and non-book materials in the library collection; lists types of library equipment needed for these services.

UNESCO DOC. CODE: FMR/CC/DBA/76/174; RP/1975–76/ 4.221.4/Rapport technique. MICROFICHE: 77fr0059. (Restricted).

282. Savitz, Gerald S.
The Libyan library development plan: a special report for the Ministry of Education and Guidance, Tripoli, Libyan Arab Republic. November 1970.

283. Schaefer, V.
Organisation des Archives nationales et d'un système de préarchivage

(records management): Républic unie du Cameroun—(mission) janvier–février 1973. March 1974. 24p., incl. bibl.

Mission report on archive administration of the national archives, including its records management, in Cameroon UR—discusses archivists and other personnel necessary; deals with the relations to former colonial powers; includes the texts of documentation/library legislation and archive legislation with reference to the national library.

UNESCO DOC. CODE: 3022/RMO.RD/DBA. MICROFICHE: 74fr0112. (Restricted).

284. Seguin, J.P.
Propositions pour la sauvegarde des manuscrits du Maroc, et en particulier de ceux de la Bibliothèque Qaraouiyine, à Fès—(mission) 30 June 1983. 29p., illus.

Keywords: preservation of cultural property; manuscripts; document preservation; library collections; Morocco—restoration; conservation techniques; library buildings; library equipment. **Identifiers:** Bibliothèque Qaraouiyine (Morocco).

UNESCO DOC. CODE: FMR/PGI/83/142; RP/1981–83/5/10.1/ 03/Rapport technique. MICROFICHE: 83fr0185. (Restricted).

285. Sewell, P.H.
Developing an information system for the Sudan—(mission) 1979. 67p., incl. bibl.

Keywords: scientific information; national information systems; information/library development; documentation centre; libraries; Sudan—information user needs; information/library co-operation; information user instruction; information/library networks; information/library personnel. **Identifiers:** National Documentation Centre (Sudan).

UNESCO DOC. CODE: FMR/PGI/79/230 (UNDP); UNDP/SUD/ 74/036/Technical report. MICROFICHE: 79fr0169. (Restricted).

286. Sewell, P.H.
Report and survey on library services in the Sudan (1960). Paris: Unesco, 1963. (Mimeographed).

UNESCO DOC. CODE: PP/SUD/CUA/3.

287. Sharify, N.
Création de l'École des sciences de l'information: Maroc—(mission) 17–31 août 1974. October 1974. 39p. (in various pagings).

Mision report on an information science training school in Morocco—examines its academic teaching personnel, educational administrative structure and curriculum development; also refers to its impact on national documentation/library development; provides educational financing and enrolment ratios.

UNESCO DOC. CODE: 3089/RMO.RD/DBA. MICROFICHE: 75fr0018. (Restricted).

288. Sharify, Nasser.
Evaluation and recommendations for the revision of the programme of Morocco's School of Information Science: Morocco—(mission) 31 December 1980. 91p., illus.

Keywords: information science training; information/library schools; educational reform; educational programmes; Morocco—university libraries; curriculum development; teacher status; enrolment; educational statistics; educational assessment; evaluation. **Identifiers:** Ecole des sciences de l'information (Morocco).

UNESCO DOC. CODE: FMR/PGI/OPS/80/280 (UNDP); UNDP/MOR/74/003/Assignment report. MICROFICHE: 81fr0092. (Restricted).

289. Sharify, Nasser.
The Pahlavi National Library of the future: a summary of its origin, its planning, its objectives and its services. New York: Pahlavi National Library Board of Consultants, 1976.

The citations for the 17-volume report on the Pahlavi National Library, prepared by over 100 experts were not available. The report is described by one of the experts in the following words:

> To plan for a national library reflecting the reality of this century, including the NATIS (National Information Systems) concept as promoted by UNESCO, and capturing the imagination of the next century, obviously required a wide variety of high expertise not possessed by any single individual. I therefore turned to all those whose specialized know-

ledge was needed for various facets of library, resources, services, programs, and facilities. With the assistance of many, and practically a worldwide search, in a three-month period over 100 experts were recruited, representing many nations and thus bringing with them a colorful diversity in concepts, principles, and practices. Harmony was achieved during a major briefing conference held for all consultants in Long Island, New York, in July 1975, before they departed for a month-long mission in Iran in August 1975.

On March 12, 1976, a 17-volume report composed of approximately 5,000 pages was officially submitted to Iran.

These included 11 volumes of position papers by consultants and a 6-volume final report of the chairman of the board of consultants, the last of which was devoted to a detailed building program.

290. Sharify, N.
Plan d'ensemble pour la création d'une école des sciences de l'information: Maroc—(mission) novembre 1973–janvier 1974. August 1974. 75p.

Mission report on the creation of a documentation/library school in Morocco for information science training—discusses its curriculum planning and its educational administrative structure; refers to the need for documentation/library personnel; also considers information systems of the country and its documentation/library network within the framework of economic and social development.

UNESCO DOC. CODE: 3072/RMO.RD/DBA. MICROFICHE: 74fr0157. (Restricted).

291. Slamecka, Vladimir.
Egyptian national system for scientific and technical information: design study. Atlanta, GA.: Georgia Institute of Technology, School of Information and Computer Science, November 1981. xiv, 131p.

Keywords: science and technology; information systems; systems analysis; Egypt—institution building; data processing; documentation; communications technology; organization development.

U.S. NATIONAL SCIENCE FOUNDATION CONTRACT NO. INT-7924187; PASA NF/EGY-0016-7-77. DOC. NO. PN-AAP-073.

292. Slamecka, Vladimir.
Manpower development for Egyptian STI services. Atlanta, GA.: Georgia Institute for Technology, School of Information and Computer Science, January 1982. v, 52p.

Keywords: science and technology; information services; manpower utilization; Egypt—national planning; personnel development; professional personnel; paraprofessionals; training methods; curriculum development.

U.S. NATIONAL SCIENCE FOUNDATION CONTRACT NO. INT-7924187; PASA NF/EGY-0016-7-77. DOC. NO. PN-AAP-153.

293. Slamecka, Vladimir.
National STI system of Egypt: implementation. Atlanta, GA.: Georgia Institute of Technology, School of Information and Computer Science, November 1981. viii, 71p.

Keywords: science and technology; information services; organization development; Egypt—institution building; information systems; management training.

U.S. NATIONAL SCIENCE FOUNDATION CONTRACT NO. INT-7924187; PASA NF/EGY-0016-7-77. DOC. NO. PN-AAP-072.

294. Slamecka, Vladimir.
Survey of scientific and technological information resoures in selected Egyptian organizations. Atlanta, GA.: Georgia Institute of Technology, School of Information and Computer Science, September 1981. vi, 88p.

Keywords: science and technology; information services; organizations; Egypt—manpower utilization; libraries; information centres; technical assistance; educational facilities; professional personnel; publishing industry.

U.S. NATIONAL SCIENCE FOUNDATION CONTRACT NO. INT-7924187; PASA NF/EGY-0016-7-77. DOC. NO. PN-AAP-156.

295. Srivastava, A.P.
Iraq: education for library science and documentation, 28 January to 27 July 1968. Paris: Unesco, 1969. 30p.

296. Srivastava, A.P.
Iraq: library training and special libraries, November 1969–May 1970. Unesco, 1970. 30p.

297. State University of New York, International Studies and World Affairs.
Book production, importation and distribution in Iran, Pakistan and Turkey: a study with regional recommendations within the context of social and economic development. Oyster Bay, N.Y.: State University of New York, December 1966. 53p.
U.S.A.I.D. CONTRACT NO. AID/CSd-1199.

298. Stobart, Raymond.
Manpower development for the University: People's Democratic Republic of Yemen—(mission) 31 May 1979. 13p.

Keywords: information/library schools; library training; information/library personnel; manpower needs; Yemen PDR—enrolment; training courses. **Identifiers:** University of Aden (Yemen PDR), Library.

UNESCO DOC. CODE: FMR/PGI/79/138; RP/1977–78/5.1.4/ Technical report. MICROFICHE: 79fr0179. (Restricted).

299. Stockhan, K.A.
The establishment of a two-year course in library and information studies: a report to the Ministry of Education in Kuwait. Kuwait: Ministry of Eduction, 1977. 19p.

300. Taylor, J.C.
Hydrogeological education and training at the University of Jordan to benefit national water resources development programmes: Hashemite Kingdom of Jordan—(mission) 6 November–5 December 1976. 28 February 1977. 17p. (in various pagings).

Mission report on higher education in hydrogeology and hydrology education in Jordan, including reference to research planning for hydrological research—recommends the establishment of a national documentation centre to organize existing documentation, as well as an automatic information storage and data retrieval system for hydrological data.

Keywords: higher education; hydrogeology; hydrology education; Jordan; research planning; hydrological research—documentation centre; information processing; data retrieval; hydrological data.

UNESCO DOC. CODE: FMR/SC/HYD/77/112; PP/1975–76/

2.233.4/End-of-assignment report. MICROFICHE: 77fr0137. (Restricted).

301. Tell, Björn V.
Pilot project for the development of a university library network: Republic of Indonesia—(mission) 27 March 1981. 78p. (in various pagings), illus. bibl.

Keywords: university libraries; information/library networks; information/library co-operation; pilot projects; Indonesia—educational planning; higher education; information/library planning; library collections; information/library personnel; library services; information/library budgets; information/library resources; library automation; information processing; information transfer; information/library facilities; information user instruction.

UNESCO DOC. CODE: FMR/PGI/OPS/81/206 (UNDP); UNDP/INS/78/057/Technical report. MICROFICHE: 81fr0130. (Restricted).

302. Tell, Björn V.
Pilot project on the development of a library network: Malaysia—(mission) 15 April–5 June 1976. 2 November 1976. 30p.

Mission report on a pilot project for the development of a documentation/library network of university libraries in Malaysia to serve as a model for documentation/library co-operation and university co-operation in the Asian region—discusses the national policy for documentation/library development, mentioning questions of acquisitions and computerized libraries; describes the status of the country's research libraries and plans for centralized cataloguing; refers to manpower needs for documentation/library personnel, and the establishment of a telex network.

UNESCO DOC. CODE: FMR/CC/DBA/76/153; RP/1975–76/4.221.3/Technical report. MICROFICHE: 77fr0082.

303. Thirion, Gérard.
Bibliothèque centrale universitaire dans le cadre du Centre national universitaire de documentation scientifique et technique: Tunisie—(mission) 13 April 1981. 33p., incl. bibl.

Keywords: university libraries; information/library centralization; information/library planning; Tunisia–information/library personnel; terminology; data analysis; library collections; information/library policy; acquisition policy; technical assistance; library buildings; information/library financing; manpower needs; information/library legislation. **Identifiers:** Université de Tunis, Bibliothèque centrale universitaire.

UNESCO DOC. CODE: FMR/PGI/OPS/81/214 (SP); SP/413/TUN/3089/Rapport technique. MICROFICHE: 81fr0213. (Restricted).

304. Thirion, Gérard.
Bibliothèque de l'Université de Dakar: République du Sénégal—(mission) 19 October 1982. 19p.

Keywords: university libraries; information/library development; Senegal—acquisitions; information/library budgets; information/library personnel; library services. **Identifiers:** Université de Dakar, Bibliothèque.

UNESCO DOC. CODE: FMR/PGI/82/164; PP/1981–83/5/10.1/05/Rapport technique. MICROFICHE: 83fr0012. (Restricted).

305. Thompson, Anthony.
'Library mission to Kuwait', *Library World*, 64 (January 1963), 179–84.

306. Thompson, Lawrence S.
A program for library development in Turkey. Ankara: Milli Egitim Basimevi, 1952.

307. Thornhill, Mary.
Development report to Ministry of Education on national library service in the Gambia. (1973?)

308. Touscoz, Jean; Lormand, Jacques.
Co-opération scientifique et technique entre les États membres de l'UDEAC—(mission régionale) 30 September 1977. 107p. (in various pagings), incl. bibl.

Mission report on the strengthening of scientific co-operation between the four member states of the Central African Customs and Economic Union (UDEAC), namely the Central African

Empire, Cameroon UR, Congo PR, and Gabon—examines the national science policy and scientific research programme of each country; identifies research priorities to be undertaken on a basis of regional co-operation; discusses the importance of scientific information and information exchange; includes an outline of the administrative structure of UDEAC and refers to the science administration of research programmes; provides statistical data.

Keywords: scientific co-operation; Central African Empire; Cameroon UR; Congo PR; Gabon—science policy; scientific research; research priorities; regional co-operation; scientific information; information exchange; administrative structure; science administration; research programmes. **Identifiers:** Union douanière et économique de l'Afrique centrale.

UNESCO DOC. CODE: FMR/SC/STP/77/195; RP/1977–78/2.1211.6/Rapport technique. MICROFICHE: 78fr0074. (Restricted).

309. U.S. Agency for International Development.
Book survey in Malaysia. Washington, D.C.: U.S.A.I.D., 1965.

310. *University instructional materials project; feasibility study.*
Cairo: U.S. Agency for International Development, Bureau for Near East, 1978. 23p.

Keywords: instructional materials; educational technology; education, higher; libraries; textbooks; Egypt.

DOC. NO. PA-AAG-440.

311. Valls, Jaime.
Project pilote pour la mécanisation des services de documentation dans les pays arabes (études preliminaire): Tunisie—(mission) 18 novembre 1975–15 janvier 1976. 25 May 1976. 23p., incl. bibl.

Mission report describing a pilot project for introducing computerized documentation at the National Documentation centre in Tunisia—describes the documentation/library operations of the centre, which specializes in social science information; emphasizes the need for more documentation/library cooperation between the country's information services; also deals with documentation training and thesaurus compilation; considers the documentation/library administration of the centre necessary to effect these changes.

UNESCO DOC. CODE: FMR/CC/DBA/76/119; RP/1975-76/2.121.2/Rapport technique. MICROFICHE: 77fr0124. (Restricted).

312. Vasarhelyi, P.
Feasibility of establishing the Arab Regional Documentation Centre—(mission) 28 March 1980. 18p. (in various pagings)

Keywords: documentation centres; information services; social science information; information and development; project design; Arab States—information/library co-operation; information users; information network; information processing; information science training; information/library personnel. **Identifiers:** Centre for Social Science Research and Documentation for the Arab Region (Egypt). Arab Regional Documentation Centre for Economic and Social Development. Centre for Documentation and Information of the Arab League. DEVSIS Africa. DEVSIS Western Asia.

UNESCO DOC. CODE: FMR/PGI/80/208 (ECWA); ECWA/Unesco/Assignment report. MICROFICHE: 80fr0095. (Restricted).

313. Vaska, Jules.
Educational planning and administration: Bangladesh—(mission) 14 August 1980. 36p., illus., incl. bibl.

Keywords: educational planning; educational administration; educational information; educational statistics; Bangladesh—educational systems; educational documentation; information/library personnel; information science training, dissemination of information. **Identifiers:** Bangladesh, Bureau of Educational Information and Statistics.

UNESCO DOC. CODE: FMR/ED/OPS/80/245 (UNDP); UNDP/BGD/74/002/Technical report. MICROFICHE: 80fr0159. (Restricted).

314. Vaughan, Anthony.
Assistance à l'ecole des sciences de l'information: Maroc—(mission) 7 octobre–30 décembre 1976. 20 April 1977. 37p. (in various pagings).

Mission report on an information science training school in Morocco with special reference to curriculum planning—provides a curriculum evaluation of the documentation/library school; mentions teaching methods and teacher training of the academic teaching personnel; also considers the school's educational administrative structure and its documentation/library facilities.

Keywords: information science training; Morocco; curriculum planning—curriculum evaluation; information/library schools; teaching methods; teacher training; academic teaching personnel; educational administrative structure; information/library facilities. **Identifiers:** École des sciences de l'information (Morocco).

UNESCO DOC. CODE: FMR/PGI/77/219 (UNDP); UNDP/MOR/74/003. MICROFICHE: 78fr0043. (Restricted).

315. Vaughan, Anthony.
La formation de documentalistes, de bibliothécaires et d'archivistes: Tunisie—(mission) 6 August 1982. 56p.

Keywords: library training; documentation training; archive science training; Tunisia—university curriculum; curriculum development; post-graudate courses; masters degrees; information/library schools; academic teaching personnel. **Identifiers:** Institut de presse et de sciences de l'information (Tunisia).

UNESCO DOC. CODE: FMR/PGI/82/136; PP/1981–83/5/10.1/05/Rapport technique. MICROFICHE: 83fr0026. (Restricted).

316. Vaughan, Anthony.
La formation de documentalistes, de bibliothécaires et l'information (IPSI): Tunisie—(mission) 31 March 1981. 49p., illus.

Keywords: information science training; information/library personnel; information/library schools; curriculum planning; curriculum evaluation; Tunisia—curriculum development; documentation centres; university libraries; manpower needs; documentalists; professional status; educational systems; educational programmes; evaluation of education; information/library administration; educational financing. **Identifiers:** Institut de presse et des sciences de l'information (Tunisia).

UNESCO DOC. CODE: FMR/PGI/81/115; RP/1979–80/5/10/1/05/Rapport technique. MICROFICHE: 81fr0106. (Restricted).

317. Vuorinen, Seppo.
Introduction of machine-readable cataloguing at the National Information and Documentation Centre: Arab Republic of Egypt—(mission) 29 December 1976–26 January 1977. 20 April 1977. 7p.

Mission report on library automation, with particular reference to the mechanization of cataloguing routines at the Egyptian National Information and Documentation Centre (NIDOC)—discusses the choice of computer software in terms of compatibility with MARC-Format and ISBD(M); recommends an information science training course for NIDOC documentation/library personnel in computerized cataloguing techniques.

Keywords: library automation; cataloguing; Egypt; Documentation Centre—computer software; compatibility; ISBD(M); information science training; information/library personnel.
Identifiers: National Information and Documentation Centre (Egypt). MARC format.

UNESCO DOC. CODE: FMR/BEP/PGI/77/144; RP/1975–76/4.221.2/Technical report. MICROFICHE: 78fr0050.

318. Wagner, Alfred.
Mise en route du service national d'archives dans le cadre du système national d'information (NATIS): Haute Volta—(mission) 21 février–6 mars 1976. 29 April 1976. 38p. (in various pagings), plans.

Mission report reviewing the reorganization of the national archives in Upper Volta within the framework of a national information system—stresses the need for the development of the archive facilities of the country, and includes plans for the building design; also examines archive legislation related to the creation of the Centre national des archives.

UNESCO DOC. CODE: FMR/CC/DBA/76/118; PP/1975–76/4.221.4/Rapport technique. MICROFICHE: 77fr0125. (Restricted).

319. Ward, Philip.
Development of a national library service: technical reports: Indonesia—(mission) April 1973–November 1974. June 1975. 3 pts. (pt. 1, Proposals for a national plan for library development;

pt. 2, Evaluation of provincial library services; pt. 3, Project findings and recommendations), incl. bibl.

Mission report on documentation/library development in Indonesia; described, in particular, the documentation/library planning of a national library service—provides a brief country report and a review of the general library situation in the country, including its public libraries, children's libraries, school libraries, research libraries, university libraries, mobile libraries and special libraries; examines the question of bibliographic control, with reference to the national bibliography; considers library training and education and documentation/library legislation; deals with national documentation centres, documentation/library networks and the national library; studies other aspects of development, such as documentation/library co-operation, documentation/library administration and book development; presents an evaluation of regional libraries and rural libraries in Indonesia, giving details on the different areas and types of libraries covered; includes documentation/library statistics for all regions concerned.

UNESCO DOC. CODE: 3180/RMO.RD/DBA PART I; 3181/RMO.RD/DBA PART II; INS/72/024 1; INS/72/024 2; INS/72/024/Terminal report. MICROFICHE: 75fr0134. (Restricted).

320. Weilbrenner, Bernard.
Réorganisation et développement des archives: Haute-Volta—(mission) octobre 1972. February 1973. 35p. (in various pagings), plan.

Mission report on the improvement of national archives in Upper Volta—reviews the present situation and outlines a 7-year plan for reorganization; refers to questions relating to records management and a classification system; considers need for training abroad of archivists, and the elaboration of legislation concerning archives and legal status of personnel; includes also a cost evaluation of the whole reorganization.

UNESCO DOC. CODE: 2849/RMO.RD/DBA. MICROFICHE: 73fr0182. (Restricted).

321. White, Neva L.
The Kabul University Library: terminal report. Kabul: University of Wyoming Project, 1966.

322. Whitenack, Carolyn I.
Report to the United States Agency for International Development on audiovisual programs of library development at the Middle East Technical University, Ankara, Turkey. Purdue University, July 1972. 133p.

323. Willemin, S.
Développement des services de bibliothèque en milieu rural: République Populaire du Bénin—(mission) 7 avril–6 juin 1978. August 1978. 15p. (in various pagings).

Keywords: library services; information/library development; rural libraries; Benin PR—library extension work; illiteracy; book production; vernacular languages; library training.

UNESCO DOC. CODE: FMR/BEP/PGI/78/134; RP/1977–78/5.1.3/Rapport de mission. MICROFICHE: 79fr0114. (Restricted).

324. Willemin, S.
Liban: développement des bibliothèques, 15 novembre 1967–31 décembre 1968. Paris: Unesco, 1969.

UNESCO DOC. CODE: 1612/BMS.RD/DBA.

325. Willemin, S.
Sénégal: développement des bibliothèque (octobre 1964–juin 1966). Paris: Unesco, 1966. 11p.

UNESCO DOC. CODE: AT/AFRICAC/4.

326. Williams, H.
Detailed specifications for the development of an educational media centre: Malaysia—(mission) October 1972. 1972. 55p., tables.

Mission report presenting specifications for the proposed educational technology training centre at Penang university of science, Malaysia, designed for teacher training and communication personnel training in the production and utilization of audiovisual aids for teaching and learning purposes—covers school building and equipment, including libraries, school workshops and school laboratory facilities and their cost; discusses the organization of training courses in educational technology and recruitment.

UNESCO DOC. CODE: 2812/RMO.RD/MC. MICROFICHE: 73fr0141. (Restricted).

327. Williamson, William L.
University library development in Indonesia: a report to the Ministry of Education and Culture, Republic of Indonesia. 18 September 1970. 19p.

328. Wilson, T.D.
Étude de faisabilité d'une enquête sur les besoins des utilisateurs dans le secteur agricole: Tunisie—(mission) March 1979. 22p., illus.

Keywords: information network; agricultural information system; rural population; information user needs; surveys feasibility studies; Tunisia. **Identifiers:** Centre national de documentation agricole (Tunisia).

UNESCO DOC. CODE: FMR/PGI/DII/117; RP/1977–78/5.13.1/ Rapport de mission. MICROFICHE: 80fr0140. (Restricted).

329. Wrong, Margaret.
Libraries: Nigeria, Gold Coast, Sierra Leone and Gambia. New York: Carnegie Corporation for the Colonial Office London, 1939. 23p.

330. Zanuttini, Francesco.
General analysis of national and provincial requirements concerning educational management information systems: Pakistan—(mission) 22 July 1982. 79p. (in various pagings), illus.

Keywords: educational management; management information systems; computer applications; Pakistan—information/library budgets; information/library co-operation; scientific personnel; educational statistics; data collection; minicomputers; questionnaires; educational projects. **Identifiers:** Pakistan, Education Dept. Management Unit for Study and Training.

UNESCO DOC. CODE: FMR/ED/OPS/82/241 (UNDP); UNDP/ PAK/77/009; UNDP/PAK/77/038; UNDP/PAK/78/008; UNDP/PAK/012; UNDP/PAK/78/048/Assignment report. MICROFICHE: 82fr0072. (Restricted).

331. Zanuttini, Francesco.
Gestion de l'éducation nationale: République populaire du Bénin—(mission) 16 novembre–1er décembre 1976. 11 March 1977. 54p. (in various pagings), illus.

Mission report analysing the educational administrative structure and procedures of the national educational system in Benin PR—outlines the present educational management and deals with problems of decentralization, information transfer and educational personnel training.

Keywords: educational administrative structure; educational systems; Benin PR—educational management; decentralization; information transfer; educational personnel training.

UNESCO DOC. CODE: FMR/ED/OPS/77/215 (PNUD); PNUD/BEN/75/006. MICROFICHE: 77fr0153. (Restricted).

332. Zanuttini, Francesco.
Revue technique des activités ayant a l'informatisation de la gestion réalisées dans le cadre du 3ème project éducation finance par la Banque Mondiale: Royaume du Maroc—(mission) 1981. 24p. (in various pagings), illus.

Keywords: management information systems; on-line information systems; information/library planning; government departments; educational systems; Morocco—systems analysis; technical assistance; technical training; recruitment; questionnaires. **Identifiers:** Morocco. Ministère de l'education nationale et de la formation des cadres, Centre informatique.

UNESCO DOC. CODE: FMR/ED/OPS/81/253 (BIRD); BIRD/700/MOR/10/Rapport de mission. MICROFICHE: 81fr0208. (Restricted).

333. Zanuttini, Francesco; Murdoch, J.
Tripartite project review (SAU/79/002) and general analysis of information needs and priorities in higher education with a view to establishing the framework for a coordinated university information system: Kingdom of Saudi Arabia—(mission) 21 January 1983. 1 v. (in various pagings), illus.

Keywords: higher education; universities; information user needs; educational information systems; feasibility studies; Saudi Arabia—educational development; educational information; data collection; data processing; project design; project management; project implementation; project evaluation. **Identifiers:** Saudi Arabia, Ministry of Higher Education.

UNESCO DOC. CODE: FMR/ED/OPS/83/201 (UNDP); UNDP/

SAU/79/002/Assignment report. MICROFICHE: 83fr0058. (Restricted).

334. Zarata, Alvan O.; Davids, Donald J.
Report of mission of the National Center for Health Statistics to Cairo, Egypt. Washington, D.C.: American Public Health Association, International Health Programs, 4 April 1983. 11p. + appendices.

Keywords: vital statistics; health data collection; Egypt—documentation; data acquisition; mortality; data processing; data transmission; information systems.

U.S.A.I.D. CONTRACT NO. AID/DSPE-c-0053. DOC. NO. PN-AAP-010.

335. Zeida, Rubén E.
Budgétisation fonctionnelle et programmation budgétaire des activités scientifiques et technologiques: Sénégal—(mission) 2–22 octobre 1977. 30 December 1977. 85p. (in various pagings), incl. bibl.

Mission report presenting a feasibility study on computer applications of budgeting procedure to scientific activities in Senegal within the framework of national science policy—identifies activities falling within the domain of science and technology and of the science budget, such as scientific personnel training, research and development and scientific information; discusses the administration of the national budget and the country's existing science administration; also deals with the methodology of computer programming and research co-ordination.

Keywords: feasibility studies; computer applications; budgeting; scientific activities; Senegal; science policy—science and technology; science budgets; scientific personnel training; research and development; scientific information; science administration; methodology; computer programming; research co-ordination.

UNESCO DOC. CODE: FMR/SC/STP/77/276 (UNDP); UNDP/SEN/74/003/Rapport technique. MICROFICHE: 78fr0131. (Restricted).

336. Zeiler, Huguette.
L'Institut culturel africain; Centre regional d'etudes, de recherche et de

documentation sur le développement culturel: Regional—(mission) 6 septembre–1 er octobre 1976. 15 February 1977. 22p.

Mission report on the establishment of a regional documentation centre for cultural research on cultural development within the Institut culturel africain to serve Africa south of the Sahara—discusses the documentation/library administration of the centre and the documentation/library personnel required; describes the cataloguing and indexing of materials on African cultures.

Keywords: documentation centre; cultural research; cultural development; Africa south of the Sahara—information/library administration; information/library personnel; cataloguing; indexing; African cultures. **Identifiers:** Institut culturel africain (Senegal).

UNESCO DOC. CODE: FMR/CC/CD/77/119; RP/1975–76/3.321/5/Rapport technique. MICROFICHE: 78fr0138. (Restricted).

337. Zell, Hans M.
The book situation in Bangladesh—(mission) 10 June–9 July 1974. March 1975. 57p., incl. bibl.

Mission report advising on a book development programme for Bangladesh—includes a study of the present situation in book production and the graphic arts, including printing paper, publishing, newspapers and periodicals as well as textbook production; recommends the strengthening of the book industry and book distribution; gives a brief outline of the educational system and the documentation/library network.

UNESCO DOC. CODE: 3143/RMO.RD/FDC. MICROFICHE: 75fr0093. (Restricted).

338. Zoghby, Samir M.
A publication survey trip to West Africa, Tunisia, France and Belgium. (Washington, D.C.): Library of Congress, General Reference and Bibliography Division. Reference Department, 1968.

Joint Author Index

The Joint Author Index lists authors who were mentioned after the first one in multi-authored reports and were not, therefore, in their appropriate alphabetical-by-author positions in the bibliography.

Albin, M.W., 232
Balquière, Henri, 260
Bonnichon, Monique, 2
Brown, Emerson L., 26, 27, 28
Byrd, Cecil K., 28
Canzonier, Walter J., 124
Cardwell, Vernon B., 254
Chevalier, H.F., 28
Clearhill, E., 73
Dandison, B.G., 28
Davids, Donald J., 334
Dobrov, Gennady M., 157
Emmerson, Harold G., 25
Francis, Simon, 19
Frase, Robert W., 26, 27
Al-Ghul, M., 169
Gottleib, H.J., 28
Green, Charles B., 154
Grobillot, Jean Louis, 78, 79, 80
Hurst, Kenneth T., 26, 27
Jacsó, Péter, 206
Kennedy, P.J., 73
Khan, Bashir Ali, 15
Kingston, J., 73
Lancour, Harold A., 98
Larson, Douglas, 272
Lormand, Jacques, 308

Mackenzie, A.G., 73
Madkour, Mohamed A., 5
Mahmoud, U.E., 232, 233
Murdoch, J., 333
Naibert, Zane E., 51, 98
Neumann, Peter H., 26, 27
Palmour, Vernon, 208
Patah, R., 92
Price, D.J.de Solla, 157
Reheem, K., 157
Rose, John B., 32
Salomonsson, Owe, 278
Schabel, Donald, 15
Schyfsma, E., 73
Serviss, Trevor K., 98
Sewell, Philip Hooper, 239
Sharify, Nasser, 25, 51
Slamecka, Valadimir, 5
Thomas, D.L., 181
Thomas, R.M., 28
Thut, I.N., 26, 27
Tiwana, Nazar, 15
Tocatlian, Jacques, 262
Vasudevan, Mullath, 6
Vorwerk, Claus, 6
Watts, Franklin, 51

Subject Index

ALECSO
  See Arab League Educational, Cultural and Scientific Organization
ALIS
  See Arab League Information System
Afghanistan, 17, 36, 82, 88, 101, 163, 321
Africa, British West, 105, 193
  See also Africa, West
Africa, East, 275, 279
Africa, French-speaking, 2, 59
Africa, West, 338
Agricultural Information System, Tunisia, 328
Agricultural libraries
  Arab States, 20
  Indonesia, 154
  Pakistan, 245
Algeria, 46, 112, 127, 214, 226, 228, 231, 243, 259, 262
Ankara University (Turkey). Faculty of Letters. Institute of Librarianship, 125
Arab Centre for the Studies of Arid Zones and Dry Lands (Syria). Documentation Unit, 20
Arab Gulf Folklore Centre (Qatar). Information Centre, 235
Arab League. Centre for Documentation and Information, 9, 10, 11, 172, 196, 197, 198, 218, 267, 276, 312
Arab League Educational, Cultural and Scientific Organization (ALECSO), 211
Arab League Information System (ALIS), 267
Arab Scientific and Technological Information Network, 224
Arab States, 4, 9, 10, 11, 90, 172, 179, 184, 196, 197, 198, 211, 218, 224, 267, 276, 312
  See also names of individual Arab countries.
Arab States Broadcasting Union. Information Unit, 196
Archive buildings
  Bourkina Faso, 318
  Guinea, 103
  Iraq, 95
  Malaysia, 89
Archive legislation
  Afghanistan, 82
  Bourkina Faso, 318, 320
  Cameroun, 283
  Lebanon, 14
  Uganda, 8
Archive science education
  Afghanistan, 82
  Africa, French-speaking, 59
  Chad, 134
  Indonesia, 182
  Lebanon, 53, 116
  Mauritania, 135
  Morocco, 39, 74, 75
  Niger, 229

126 Subject Index

Senegal, 59, 212, 229, 260
Sudan, 271
Tunisia, 315, 316
Turkey, 44
Uganda, 8
Archives
Afghanistan, 82
Algeria, 243
Bourkina Faso, 318, 320
Cameroun, 50, 111, 222, 283
Chad, 134
Gabon, 110, 234
Iraq, 95, 244
Lebanon, 14, 53, 76
Libya, 62, 238
Malaysia, 89, 100
Mali, 33
Mauritania, 135
Morocco, 245
Oman, 181
Sierra Leone, 34
Somalia, 200
Tunisia, 107
Turkey, 44
Uganda, 8
Archives, audiovisual
Arab States, 4
Audiovisual services
Arab States, 4
Libya, 106
Malaysia, 326
Saudi Arabia, 97
Turkey, 322
United Arab Emirates, 30
Bahrain, 13, 123
Bahrain. Ministry of Education, 13
Bangladesh, 3, 176, 177, 183, 236, 313, 337
Bangladesh. Bureau of Educational Information and Statistics, 313
Bangladesh. National Book Centre, 3
Bénin (Dahomey), 46, 58, 85, 102, 188, 189, 261, 323, 331
Bénin. Bibliothèque nationale, 261
Bénin. Centre de formation administrative et de perfectionnement, 188
Bibliographical services
Pakistan, 109
Book industry
Bangladesh, 3, 337

Egypt, 65, 185
Gambia, 180
Guinea, 114
Indonesia, 28, 29, 81, 241
Iran, 98, 192, 297
Malaysia, 309
Mali, 129
Morocco, 115
Pakistan, 51, 142, 297
Sierra Leone, 84, 143
Tunisia, 338
Turkey, 25, 26, 297
West Africa, 338
Bourkina Faso (Upper Volta), 46, 58, 85, 207, 263, 318, 320
British West Africa
See Africa, British West
Cameroun, 46, 50, 58, 60, 85, 111, 166, 167, 222, 283, 308
Cameroun. Archives nationale, 283
Centralized book processing, Iran, 152
Centre for Social Science Research and Documentation for the Arab Region (Egypt), 312
Centre régional de documentation et d'information scientifiques en ecologie tropicale (Cameroun), 166
Centre régional de documentation du MAB (Cameroun), 167
Chad, 46, 58, 85, 134
College libraries, Pakistan, 183
Comoros, 45
Comoros. Centre national de documentation et de recherches, 45
Computer science education, Sudan, 277
Dahomey see Bénin
Documentation education
Iraq, 295
Senegal, 212, 260
Tunisia, 315, 316
Uganda, 279
Documentation services
Africa, French-speaking, 2
Algeria, 112, 127, 228
Arab States, 10, 20, 184, 211, 276, 312
Bahrain, 13

Bangladesh, 177, 313
Bénin, 58, 85
Bourkina Faso, 58, 85, 263
Cameroun, 50, 58, 85, 166, 222
Chad, 58, 85
Comoros, 45
Egypt, 190, 269, 270, 291
Gabon, 110, 132
Guinea, 58, 85
Guinea Bissau, 221
Gulf States, 141, 155
Indonesia, 144, 146, 170, 217, 225
Iran, 52, 131, 210
Iraq, 113, 156, 206, 223, 247
Jordan, 128, 300
Lebanon, 49, 66, 99
Libya, 238
Mali, 58, 85, 168
Mauritania, 159
Morocco, 55, 228, 266
Niger, 58, 85, 203
Pakistan, 48
Qatar, 138
Saudi Arabia, 54
Senegal, 31, 56, 273, 336
Somalia, 86
Sudan, 171, 219, 239, 256, 285
Syria, 90
Tunisia, 18, 64, 77, 130, 199, 228, 242, 311, 328
Uganda, 8
United Arab Emirates, 155
East Africa
See Africa, East
East African School of Librarianship
See Makerere University (Uganda). East African School of Librarianship
École des sciences de l'information, Rabat (Morocco), 39, 74, 75, 94, 126, 191, 287, 288, 290, 314
Educational information
Algeria, 112, 214
Bahrain, 13
Bangladesh, 313
Bénin, 331
Indonesia, 81
Iraq, 96
Kuwait, 204
Lebanon, 35
Morocco, 332

Pakistan, 330
Saudi Arabia, 333
Egypt, 5, 65, 68, 69, 119, 136, 137, 157, 173, 175, 185, 190, 208, 211, 230, 232, 233, 248, 251, 269, 270, 272, 280, 291, 292, 293, 294, 310, 317, 334.
Egypt. National Bibliographic and Scientific Computer Centre, 68
Egypt. National Information and Documentation Centre, 190, 269, 270, 317
Egypt. National Library, 69, 173, 175, 230
Engineering libraries, Iran, 145
Federation of Arab Scientific Research Councils, 224
Fès (Morocco). Bibliotheque Qaraouiyine, 284
Film libraries, Gulf States, 141
French-speaking Africa
See Africa, French-speaking
Gabon, 46, 110, 132, 133, 234, 308
Gabon. Archives nationale, 234
Gabon. Bibliothèque nationale, 110
Gambia, 105, 108, 180, 193, 307, 329
Garyounis University (Libya), 70
Gondi Shahpoor University (Iran)
See Jundi Shahpur University (Iran)
Guinea, 58, 85, 103, 114
Guinea. Archives nationale, 103
Guinea. Bibliothèque nationale, 103
Guinea-Bissau, 221
Guinea-Bissau. Centre de documentation, L'études et de recherches en matière culturelle, 221
Gulf States, 123, 141, 155
Gulf Vision System, Riyadh, Saudi Arabia, 141
Hacettepe University (Turkey). Department of Library Science, 120
Hasanuddin University (Indonesia) Library, 225
Health information systems, Egypt, 334
Health science libraries, Indonesia, 146

Human Settlements Information
  System, Indonesia, 225
ISTIS
  See Iranian Scientific and
    Technological Information
    System
Indonesia, 28, 29, 32, 81, 91, 92, 140,
  144, 146, 154, 164, 170, 182, 216,
  217, 225, 241, 246, 278, 301, 319,
  327
Indonesia. National Scientific and
  Technological Documentation
  Centre, 225
Information/library manpower
  See Library manpower
Information science education
  Algeria, 262
  Arab States, 10, 11, 172, 198
  Bénin, 188, 189
  Egypt, 136, 211
  Gabon, 133
  Indonesia, 225
  Iraq, 206
  Jordan, 12
  Morocco, 3, 74, 75, 94, 126, 191,
    262, 287, 288, 290, 314
  Senegal, 260
  Tunisia, 18, 262
Information services
  Algeria, 231
  Arab States, 4, 9, 196, 267
  Egypt, 5, 248, 251, 272, 280
  Gulf States, 235
  Indonesia, 32
  Jordan, 6, 12, 16
  Lebanon, 35
  Mali, 209
  Niger, 63
  Saudi Arabia, 78, 79, 80
  Sierra Leone, 213
  Sudan, 71
Information transfer
  Bahrain, 123
  Gulf States, 123
  Indonesia, 32
  Iraq, 113, 123
  Kuwait, 123
  Oman, 123
  Pakistan, 87
  Qatar, 123
  Saudi Arabia, 123
  Senegal, 57
  United Arab Emirates, 123
Information user needs
  Africa, French-speaking, 2
  Arab States, 9, 11, 184
  Egypt, 280
  Gulf States, 235
  Indonesia, 32, 170, 225
  Iraq, 247
  Jordan, 16
  Lebanon, 49
  Saudi Arabia, 333
  Senegal, 31, 56
  Somalia, 86
  Sudan, 285
  Syria, 90
  Tunisia, 328
  Uganda, 258
Institut africain de développement
  économique et de planification
  (Senegal). Bibliothèque, 37
Institut culturel africain (Senegal),
  336
Institut de presse et de sciences de
  l'information (Tunisia), 315,
  316
Institut national d'études et de
  recherches du bâtiment
  (Algeria), 231
Iran, 52, 98, 131, 145, 147, 148, 149,
  150, 151, 152, 153, 165, 192, 201,
  210, 268, 289
Iran. National Library, 147, 289
Iranian Scientific and Technological
  Information System (ISTIS),
  268
Iraq, 95, 96, 113, 123, 156, 178, 206,
  223, 244, 247, 295, 296
Iraq. Council of Scientific Research.
  Scientific Documentation
  Centre, 206, 223
Iraq. National Library, 178
Jordan, 6, 12, 16, 128, 179, 240, 264,
  300
Jordan. Ministry of Information.
  Directorate of Press and
  Publications, 12
Jundi Shahpur University (Iran),
  149, 201
Kabul University Library
  (Afghanistan), 88, 321

Subject Index 129

King Abdulaziz University (Saudi Arabia), 19, 21
King Saud University (Saudi Arabia), 97
Kuwait, 22, 43, 123, 204, 237, 299, 305
Kuwait University, 22
Law libraries
  Afghanistan, 36
  Uganda, 40, 41, 42
  Lebanon, 14, 35, 49, 66, 76, 99, 116, 179, 186, 202, 324
Lebanon. Centre for Educational Research and Development, 35
Lebanon. National Archives, 14, 53
Legal deposit, Cameroun, 111
Libraries
  Afghanistan, 163
  Africa, British West, 105, 193
  Algeria, 226
  Bénin, 102
  Cameroun, 222
  Egypt, 5, 119, 137, 310
  Gabon, 110
  Gambia, 105, 193, 329
  Iran, 150
  Iraq, 178
  Lebanon, 324
  Libya, 118
  Pakistan, 109
  Senegal, 325
  Sierra Leone, 105, 193, 329
  Tunisia, 61, 252
  Yemen (A.R.), 104
Libraries for the blind, Malaysia, 38
Library automation
  Africa, French-speaking, 2
  Arab States, 9, 11, 22, 276
  Cameroun, 167
  Egypt, 68, 69, 173, 175, 190, 317
  Iraq, 206
  Malaysia, 205
  Morocco, 266
  Tunisia, 174
Library buildings
  Algeria, 46
  Bénin, 46
  Bourkina Faso, 46
  Cameroun, 46
  Chad, 46
  Gabon, 46

Guinea, 103
Iran, 147, 148
Mali, 46
Mauritania, 46
Morocco, 46
Niger, 46
Pakistan, 48
Qatar, 1
Senegal, 46
Tunisia, 46
Yemen (A.R.), 47
Library collections, Arab States, 218
Library legislation
  Bangladesh, 183
  Cameroun, 283
  Comoros, 45
  Pakistan, 183
  Somalia, 220
Library manpower
  Algeria, 46
  Arab States, 9, 10, 11
  Bahrain, 13
  Bangladesh, 177
  Bénin, 46
  Bourkina Faso, 46
  Cameroun, 46
  Chad, 46
  Comoros, 45
  Egypt, 292
  Gabon, 46
  Indonesia, 164
  Lebanon, 35
  Mali, 46
  Mauritania, 46
  Morocco, 7, 46
  Niger, 46
  Pakistan, 158
  Senegal, 31, 46
  Tunisia, 46
  Yemen (P.D.R.), 298
Library networks
  Africa, French-speaking, 2
  Indonesia, 225, 301
  Malaysia, 302
  Senegal, 227
Library science education
  Algeria, 46
  Bangladesh, 183
  Bénin, 46
  Bourkina Faso, 46
  Cameroun, 46, 111

130 Subject Index

Chad, 46
Egypt, 119, 136, 137, 232, 233
Gabon, 46
Iran, 98
Iraq, 295, 296
Kuwait, 22, 299
Lebanon, 35, 116
Mali, 46
Mauritania, 46
Morocco, 46, 94
Niger, 46
Pakistan, 183
Senegal, 46, 212, 260
Tunisia, 18, 46, 315, 316
Uganda, 195, 275
Turkey, 120, 125
Yemen (P.D.R.), 298
Library services
    Afghanistan, 17
    Arab States, 179
    Bénin, 323
    Bourkina Faso, 263
    Egypt, 186
    Gambia, 108, 307
    Indonesia, 81, 91, 140, 319
    Jordan, 179, 240
    Kuwait, 305
    Lebanon, 179, 186, 202
    Libya, 238, 282
    Malaysia, 38
    Mali, 194
    Pakistan, 51, 87, 93
    Senegal, 37
    Somalia, 220, 265
    Sudan, 239, 286
    Syria, 179
    Turkey, 25, 27, 306
Libya, 23, 62, 70, 106, 118, 238, 282
MARC System, Malaysia, 205
Maghreb, 262
Makerere University (Uganda). East African School of Librarianship, 195, 275, 279
Malaysia, 38, 89, 100, 205, 302, 309, 326
Malaysia. National Archives, 89
Malaysia. National Library, 205
Maldives, 274
Maldives. National Library, 274
Mali, 33, 46, 58, 85, 129, 168, 194, 207, 209, 257

Manuscript collections
    Mali, 168
    Mauritania, 161, 162
    Morocco, 284
    Oman, 181
    Tunisia, 107
    Turkey, 67, 281
    Yemen (A.R.), 47, 169
    See also Rare book collections
Mauritania, 46, 135, 159, 160, 161, 162, 207
Mauritania. Archives nationale, 135
Mauritania. Bibliothèque nationale, 160, 161, 162
Middle East Technical University (Turkey), 187, 258, 322
Morocco, 7, 39, 46, 55, 74, 75, 94, 115, 121, 126, 191, 228, 245, 262, 284, 287, 288, 290, 314, 332
Morocco. Centre nationale de documentation, 266
Morocco. Ministère de l'éducation nationale et de la formation des cadres. Centre informatique, 332
NATIS
    See National Information System
National Archival Training School (Indonesia), 182
National bibliographies
    Cameroun, 111
    Indonesia, 319
    Tunisia, 174
National information policy
    Algeria, 127
    Egypt, 5
    Jordan, 12
National Information System (NATIS)
    Afghanistan, 101
    Algeria, 127
    Bénin, 188
    Bourkina Faso, 318
    Cameroun, 111
    Egypt, 269, 270
    Gabon, 110
    Indonesia, 144, 319
    Iran, 268, 289
    Iraq, 113, 247
    Jordan, 128
    Libya, 238
    Pakistan, 15, 87

Subject Index

Qatar, 138
Senegal, 227
Somalia, 220
Sudan, 227, 285
Tunisia, 18
Uganda, 253
National Institute of Oceanology Library (Indonesia), 216, 225
National Libraries
  Bénin, 261
  Cameroun, 111, 283
  Egypt, 69, 173, 175, 230
  Gambia, 307
  Guinea, 103
  Indonesia, 92, 319
  Iran, 147, 268, 289
  Iraq, 178
  Malaysia, 205
  Maldives, 274
  Mauritania, 160, 161, 162
  Pakistan, 87, 183
  Somalia, 220, 255
  Tunisia, 107, 174
National Packet Switching Network (Indonesia), 32
Niger, 46, 58, 63, 85, 203, 207, 229
Niger River Commission, 58, 85
Oman, 123, 181
Packet Satellite Data Network, 32
Pahlavi University Library (Iran), 148
Pakistan, 15, 48, 51, 83, 87, 93, 109, 142, 158, 183, 254, 330
Pakistan. Education Department. Management Unit for Study and Training, 330
Pakistan Scientific and Technological Information Centre, 48
Penang University of Science (Malaysia), 326
Public libraries
  Bangladesh, 183, 236
  Indonesia, 164
  Kuwait, 237
  Pakistan, 15, 87, 183
Publishing
  See Book industry
Punjab University Library (Pakistan), 83
Qatar, 1, 73, 117, 123, 138, 235
Qatar. Ministry of Education, 138

Rare book collections
  Yemen (A.R.), 47
  See also Manuscript collections
Regional co-operation
  Africa, 166, 167
  Africa, East, 275, 279
  Africa, French-speaking, 31
  Arab States, 90
  Asia, South East, 32
  Maghreb, 262
Riyadh University
  See King Saud University
Rural information system, Pakistan, 15
Rural libraries
  Bénin, 323
  Indonesia, 319
  Pakistan, 15, 87
Saudi Arabia, 19, 21, 54, 78, 79, 80, 97, 123, 333
Saudi Arabia. Centre for Statistical Data and Educational Documentation, 54
Saudi Arabia. Ministry of Foreign Affairs. Computer Control Microfilm Search System, 78, 79, 80
Saudi Arabia. Ministry of Higher Education, 333
School libraries
  Kuwait, 43, 237
  Mali, 257
  Morocco, 7
  Uganda, 139
Scientific information
  Algeria, 228
  Bangladesh, 176, 177
  Bourkina Faso, 207
  Cameroun, 308
  Egypt, 157, 294
  Gabon, 133, 308
  Iraq, 156, 223
  Mali, 207
  Mauritania, 207
  Morocco, 228
  Niger, 203, 207
  Senegal, 207, 249, 250, 335
  Tunisia, 228
  West African Economic Community, 207
Scientific information systems
  Africa, French-speaking, 2

Subject Index

Arab States, 9, 11, 172, 197, 198, 224
Cameroun, 60, 166, 167
Egypt, 208, 291, 292, 293
Indonesia, 217, 225, 246, 278
Iran, 268
Jordan, 12, 264
Morocco, 55, 121
Pakistan, 48
Senegal, 31, 57, 122
Sudan, 24, 72, 219
Syria, 90, 124
Scientific libraries
　Indonesia, 216
　Pakistan, 158
Senegal, 31, 37, 46, 56, 57, 59, 122, 207, 212, 227, 229, 249, 250, 260, 273, 304, 325, 335, 336
Senegal. Centre national de documentation scientifique et technique, 56, 273
Senegal. Réseau national de l'information scientifique et technique, 227
Sierra Leone, 34, 84, 105, 143, 193, 213, 319
Sierra Leone. National Book Development Council, 84
Somalia, 86, 200, 220, 255, 265
Somalia. Ministry of National Planning. Documentation Centre, 86
Somalia. National Library, 220, 255
Sudan, 24, 71, 72, 171, 215, 219, 239, 256, 271, 277, 285, 286
Sudan. Ministry of Foreign Affairs. Documentation Centre, 256
Sudan. National Computer Centre, 277
Sudan. National Documentation Centre, 71, 72, 171, 219, 285
Syria, 20, 90, 124, 179
Syria. Marine Sciences Centre, 124
Teheran Book Processing Centre (TEBROC), Iran, 152
Textbooks
　Egypt, 65, 137, 310
　Gambia, 180
　Sierra Leone, 84
　Tunisia, 18, 46, 61, 64, 77, 107, 130, 174, 199, 228, 242, 252, 262, 303, 311, 315, 316, 328, 338
Tunisia. Archives générales, 107
Tunisia. Bibliothèque nationale, 107, 174
Tunisia. Centre de documentation nationale, 64, 242
Tunisia. Centre national de documentation agricole, 311, 328
Turkey, 25, 26, 27, 44, 67, 120, 125, 187, 258, 281, 306, 322
Turkey. Basbakanlik Archives, 44
Training Centre for Archival Technicians (Sudan), 271
Uganda, 8, 40, 41, 42, 139, 195, 253, 275, 279
Uganda. National Archives, 8
Uganda. National Documentation Centre, 8
United Arab Emirates, 30, 123, 155
Universitè de Dakar (Sénégal). Biblioghèque, 304
Universitè de Dakar (Sénégal). Écoles des bibliothecaires, archivistes et documentalistes, 212, 229, 260
Universitè de Tunis. Bibliothèque centrale, 303
Universitè libanaise. Faculté d'information et de documentation, 53
Universitè nationale (Bénin), 189
University libraries
　Afghanistan, 88, 321
　Algeria, 46, 259
　Bangladesh, 183
　Bénin, 46
　Bourkina Faso, 46
　Cameroun, 46
　Chad, 46
　Egypt, 232, 233
　Gabon, 46
　Indonesia, 301, 327
　Iran, 148, 149, 151, 153, 165, 201
　Iraq, 113
　Jordan, 6, 16
　Libya, 70
　Malaysia, 205, 302
　Mali, 46
　Mauritania, 46
　Morocco, 46, 191
　Niger, 46

Pakistan, 83, 183
Qatar, 1, 73, 117
Saudi Arabia, 19, 21
Senegal, 46, 304
Sudan, 215
Tunisia, 46, 303
Turkey, 67, 187, 258, 281, 322
Yemen (P.D.R.), 298
University of Aden (Yemen, P.D.R.).
  Library, 298
University of Baghdad (Iraq).
  Educational Research Centre, 96
University of Cairo (Egypt), 232
University of Gezira (Sudan).
  Library, 215
University of Istanbul (Turkey).
  Central Library, 67, 281
University of Minia (Egypt), 233
University of Qatar (Qatar), 1, 117

University of Qatar (Qatar). Faculty
  of Science, 73
University of Teheran (Iran), 153,
  165
University of Teheran (Iran).
  Institute of Co-operative
  Research and Studies Library,
  151
Upper Volta
  See Bourkina Faso
West Africa
  See Africa, West
West African Economic Community,
  207
Yarmouk University (Jordan), 6, 16
Yemen Arab Republic, 47, 104, 169
Yemen, People's Democratic
  Republic of, 298

Title Index

ALDOC manpower requirements and development: League of Arab States—(mission). 172
ALDOC staff training programme: League of Arab States, Tunis—(mission). 10
Abstracting services, National Documentation Centre, Khartoum: Sudan—(mission). 171
Activités reprographiques du Centre national de documentation scientifique et technique: Sénégal—(mission). 273
Advisory mission on preparation of a contract with Al-Kabir Trading Co. for delivery of a microform system: Saudi Arabia—(mission). 78
Afghan library development plan... prepared for H.E. Dr. Abdul Madjid, Minister of Education. 163
African law libraries: a survey of current needs: a report of the Project for the Staffing of African Institutions of Legal Education and Research (SAILER). 40
African law libraries, Kenya–Uganda–Zambia; a report to SAILER. 41
Agricultural research system of Pakistan: the report of the Minnesota Reconnaissance Team. 254
Algérie: archives publiques (avril–juillet 1964). 243
Ankara University, Faculty of Letters, Institute of Librarianship. (Report to) Members of the ALA Committee, 12 March 1956. 125
Arab Gulf States Folklore Centre: establishment of an information centre: Qatar—(mission). 235
Arab Republic of Egypt: mechanisation of the catalogues of the National Library, October 1970–April 1971. 173
Archival training: Republic of Indonesia—(mission). 182
Assistance à l'École des science de l'information: Maroc—(mission) 26 mars–26 juillet 1975. 126
Assistance à l'École des sciences de l'information: Maroc—(mission). 191
Assistance à l'École des sciences de l'information: Maroc—(mission) 7 octobre–30 décembre 1976. 314
Assistance préparatoire a l'Institut national d'études et de recherches du bâtiment: Algérie—(mission). 231
Atelier de restauration à la Bibliothèque centrale de l'Université d' Istanbul: Turquie—(mission). 67
Automation in the National Bibliographic and Scientific Computer Centre: Arab Republic of Egypt—(mission). 68

Title Index

Automation in the National Library of Egypt: The Arab Republic of Egypt—(mission). 69

L'Automatisation des catalogues de la Bibliothèque nationale: Tunisie—(mission) 10 janvier–9 mars 1977. 174

Bangladesh public library survey: final report. 236

Bibliothèque centrale universitaire dans le cadre du Centre national universitaire de documentation scientifique et technique: Tunisie—(mission). 303

La Bibliothèque de l'Institut africain de développement économique et de planification—(mission): évaluation et recommendations. 37

Bibliothèque de l'Université de Dakar: République de Sénégal—(mission). 304

Bibliothèque Nationale, Bénin: rapport d'une mission... 15–19 juillet, 1976. 261

Bibliothèque nationale et archives générales; protection physique des manuscrits et des fonds d'archives: Tunisie—(mission) décembre 1973. 107

Les Bibliothèques scolaires au Maroc—(mission). 7

Les bibliothèques universitaires: Algérie—(mission). 259

Book development: Gambia—(mission) 1–31 March 1976. 180

Book development: Indonesia—(mission) September–December 1973. 241

Book production, importation and distribution in Iran; a study of needs with recommendations within the context of social and economic development. 98

Book production, importation and distribution in Iran, Pakistan and Turkey: a study with regional recommendations within the context of social and economic development. 297

Book production, importation, and distribution in Pakistan; a study of needs with recommendations within the context of social and economic development. 51

Book production, importation and distribution in Turkey; a study of needs with recommendations within the context of social and economic development. 25

The book situation in Bangladesh—(mission) 10 June–9 July 1974. 337

Book survey in Malaysia. 309

Book survey team report on libraries in Iran. 192

Books as tools for national growth and development; a case study of the use of books in Turkey. 27

Books as tools for Turkish national growth; a study and evaluation of the book industry in Turkey. 26

Books in the Republic of Guinea. 114

Broad system outline for ALDOC: League of Arab States—(mission). 11

Budgétisation fonctionnelle et programmation budgétaire des activités scientifiques et technologiques: Sénégal—(mission) 2–22 octobre 1977. 335

Centre de documentation, d'études et de recherches en matière culturelle: République de Guinée-Bissau—(mission). 221

Centre de documentation du Ministère de l'information: Iran—(mission) juin–juillet 1972. 210

Centre de documentation et d'études sur le développement culturel: Tunisie—(mission). 130

Centre de documentation et d'information sur le développement: Liban—(mission) 10 janvier–9 mai 1975. Résultats et recommendations du project. 49

Centre de documentation et recherches Ahmad Baba: Mali—(mission) 3–14 février 1974. 168

Centre de documentation sur le développement culturel: Iran—(mission) 4 Novembre–16 décembre 1973. 131

Title Index 137

Centre d'études, de recherches et de documentation sur le développement culturel: Republique gabonaise—(mission) 7 juin–16 juillet 1976. 132

Le Centre de planification de la recherche scientifique et technique: Sénégal—(mission) janvier 1972. 249

Centre for Statistical Data and Educational Documentation, Riyadh: Saudi Arabia—(mission): project findings and recommendations. 54

Centre national de documentation du Maroc—(mission). Résultats et recommendations du project. 55

Centre national de documentation économique et sociale, Alger—(mission) 15 juin–14 juillet 1976. 127

Le Centre national de documentation et de recherches: Les Comores—(mission). 45

Centre national de documentation; rapport préliminaire sur le project de mécanisation des procédés de recherche documentaire (1971–1975): Maroc—(mission) 3 mars–20 avril 1974. 266

Centre national de documentation scientifique et technique: Sénégal—(mission). 56

Centre national de planification de la recherche scientifique et technologique: Sénégal—(mission). Rapport sur les résultats du project. 57

Centre of information and exploitation of scientific and technical documentation concerning the natural resources of the Niger River Basin: Niger River Commission (Cameroon, Chad, Dahomey, Guinea, Ivory Coast, Mali, Niger, Nigeria and Upper Volta)—(mission). Report on project results; conclusion and recommendations. 58

Centre régional de documentation et d'information scientifiques en écologie tropicale: République Unie du Cameroun—(mission) 5–15 août 1978. 166

Centre régional de formation d'archivistes, Dakar: Regional—(mission). Résultats et recommendations du project. 59

Centre régional de formation d'archivistes, Dakar: Sénégal—(mission) 1 er janvier 1972–1 er août 1973. 229

Circulation of the printed media: Arab states—(mission) 29 May–24 June 1977. 123

The collection and use of research project information: The Democratic Republic of the Sudan—(mission). 71

Collection building: League of Arab States—(mission). 218

Computerization of ALDOC activities: League of Arab States—(mission). 276

Conservation of ancient manuscripts: Sultanate of Oman—(mission). 181

Construction d'un complexe documentaire Archives nationales—Bibliothèque nationale: Guinée—(mission). 103

Construction of a national archives building: Iraq—(mission). 95

Co-opération régionale pour la formation des spécialistes de l'information au Maghreb: vers l'établissement d'une école régionale: Maroc, Algérie et Tunisie—(mission) 14–21 juin 1974. 262

Co-opération scientifique et technique entre les États membres de l'UDEAC—(mission regionale). 308

Co-opération with Garyounis University: the Socialist People's Libyan Arab Jamahiriya—(mission) 29 March–5 April 1978. 70

Création de l'École des sciences de l'information: Maroc—(mission) 17–31 août 1974. 287

Création du Centre de documentation et d'etudes de Carthage: Tunisie—

(mission) 4 septembre–4 octobre 1975. 199
La création du réseau national de l'information scientifique et technique du Sénégal—(mission). 227
Création d'un centre de documentation 'Campagne archéologique pour Carthage': Tunisie—(mission) décembre 1974. 77
Création d'un service de restauration et de reprographic à la Bibliothèque centrale universitaire d'Instanbul: Turquie—(mission) 24 octobre–23 novembre 1976. 281
Création d'un service national d'archives: Tchad—(mission) décembre 1972–février 1973. 134
Création d'un système régional d'échanges d'information à caractère scientifique et pratique dans le domaine des ressources en eau: Algérie, Maroc et Tunisie—(mission). 228
Création d'une infrastructure nationale des archives, des bibliothèques et de la documentation: Gabon—(mission). 110
La création et le développement d'une unité de documentation: Centre arabe d'étude sur les zones arides et les terres fermes (ACSAD)—(mission). 20
Current problems in science and technology policy: Arab Republic of Egypt—(mission) May 1972. 157
Department of Documentation and Information of the Arab League Educational, Cultural and Scientific Organization (ALECSO): Egypt—(mission) 8 November–27 December 1972. 211
Department of Librarianship and Archival Studies and University of Cairo libraries; fact resource paper and evaluation and recommendations. 232
Design of a central library for rare books, San'a: Yemen Arab Republic—(mission) 23 March–12 April 1978. 47
Design of PASTIC (Pakistan Science and Technology Information Centre) in Islamabad—(mission) 2–27 August 1977. 48
Detailed specifications for the development of an educational media centre: Malaysia—(mission) October 1972. 326
Deuxième cycle d'études a l'École de bibliothécaires, archivistes et documentalistes de l'Université de Dakar (EBAD): La République du Sénégal—(mission). 260
Developing an information system for the Sudan—(mission). 285
Developing the textbook industry and the National Book Development Council: Sierra Leone—(mission). 84
Development and modernization of the Basbakanlik Arsir: Turkey—(mission). 44
Development of a national library service: technical reports: Indonesia—(mission) April 1973–November 1974. 319
Development of a school and public libraries network: Kuwait—(mission) 1–31 December 1974. 237
Development of documentation and academic library services: Iraq—(mission) 3 November–30 December 1976. 113
Development of documentation, library and archives serivces: Libyan Arab Republic—(mission) 2–30 May 1976. 238
Development of library and documentation services: Democratic Republic of the Sudan—(mission) March 1972. 239
Development of marine science libraries in Indonesia—(mission) 31 October 1979. 216
Development of public library services: Indonesia—(mission) 28 May–23 June 1976. 164
Development of school libraries: Uganda—(mission) 31 December 1978. 139
Development of services in the National Library: Somalia—(mission). 255

Development of the archives and records management programme: Malaysia—(mission). 100
Development of the Bangladesh National Scientific and Technical Documentation Centre (BANSDOC)—(mission) 28 December 1974–27 January 1975. 177
Development of the National Archives and the National Documentation Centre: Uganda—(mission). 8
Development of the National Documentation Centre: Hashemite Kingdom of Jordan—(mission).128
Development of the national education programme: Indonesia—(mission). Project findings and recommendations. 81
Development of the national register of research: Democratic Republic of the Sudan—(mission). 72
Development of the Scientific Documentation Centre: Iraq—(mission). 223
Development of the Yarmouk University: Hashemite Kingdom of Jordan—(mission). 6
Development project for the National Library: the Republic of Maldives—(mission). 274
Development report ot Ministry of Education on national library service in the Gambia. 307
Developmental book activities and needs in Indonesia, prepared for the U.S. Agency for International Development. 28
Développement des services de bibliothèque en milieu rural: République Populaire du Bénin—(mission) 7 avril–6 juin 1978. 323
Documentation and Analysis Centre for the Niger River Commission: Regional—(mission). Project findings and recommendations. 85
Documentaton and library services of the Ministry of Information: Hashemite Kingdom of Jordan—(mission). 12
Documentation at the Ministry of Education: State of Qatar—(mission). 138
Documentation Centre—Ministry of National Planning: Somalia—(mission), Project findings and recommendations. 86
Documentation Centre of the Ministry of Foreign Affairs: Sudan—(mission) June 1972–March 1973). 256
Documentation évènementielle: la pratique de l'indexation au Centre de documentation nationale, Tunis: Tunisie—(mission). 64
East Africa: East African School of Librarianship, March 1963–December 1964. 195
East African School of Librarianship; a course in documentation and recommendations for curriculum: Uganda—(mission) 7 August–6 September 1975. 279
East African School of Librarianship: Uganda—(mission) July 1968–November 1972. 275
Eastern Islands agricultural education (Indonesia). 154
École des sciences de l'information—Maroc—(mission). Résultats et recommendations du projet. 8 December 1981. 94
Education concerning the problems associated with the use of drugs: Sierra Leone—(mission). 213
Educational and vocational guidance in secondary schools in Kuwait—(mission). 204
Educational books for the needs of Morocco: survey report and recommendations, August 1, 1965. 115
Educational planning and administration: Bangladesh—(mission). 313
Educational Research Centre, University of Baghdad: Iraq—(mission) 1 July 1973–31 December 1975: Project findings and recommendations. 96
Educational Technology Centre, College of Education, Riyadh University (previously known as Educational Research Centre): Saudi Arabia—(mission). 97
Egypt phase II of a project concerned

with population information, education and communication. 248
Egyptian national system for scientific and technical information: alternatives for library collection development. 208
Egyptian national system for scientific and technical information: design study. 291
Enseignement de l'archivistique à l'École des sciences de l'information: Maroc—(mission). 39
Enseignement technique et professionnel: services d'information et de documentation; etudes de cas, 1: Liban. 99
The establishment of a film and video production unit: film-video and photographic archive and resources centre: Regional—(mission) 10–18 December 1976. 4
Establishment of a microfilm section at the King Abdul Aziz University, Jeddah: Saudi Arabia—(mission) December 1972–February 1973. 21
Establishment of a National Archives Service: Afghanistan—(mission) November–December 1974. 82
Establishment of a National Computer Centre: Democratic Republic of Sudan—(mission). 277
Establishment of a technical training centre in archival restoration and reprography: Democratic Republic of the Sudan—(mission). 271
The establishment of a two-years course in library and information studies: a report to the Ministry of Education in Kuwait. 299
Establishment of an information system at Yarmouk University: Hashemite Kingdom of Jordan—(mission). 16
Étude de faisabilité d'un Centre national de documentation scientifique et technique: Sénégal—(mission) 4 novembre–1 er décembre 1974. 31
Étude de faisabilité d'une enquête sur les besoins des utilisateurs dans le secteur agricole: Tunisie—(mission). 328

Étude des conditions d'implantation à Yaoundé d'un Centre régional de documentation du MAB: République Unie du Cameroun—(mission) 16 janvier–5 février 1978. 167
Étude des termes de référence d'un système d'information scientifique et technologique au Cameroun. 60
Evaluation and recommendations for the revision of the programme of Morocco's School of Information Science: Morocco—(mission). 288
Évaluation du project de démarrage du Réseau sahélien d'information et de documentation scientifiques et techniques: Comité permanent inter-États de lutte contre la sécheresse au Sahel—(mission). 2
Evaluation of ancient books and manuscripts: Yemen Arab Republic—(mission) September 1971. 169
Faculty of Science, University of Qatar—(mission) 73
Feasibility of establishing the Arab Regional Documentation Centre—(mission). 312
Feasibility study on the proposed Arab Regional Centre for Communication Research and Documentation. 184
Final report of the School Library Advisor on work with National Pedagogical Institute, Ministry of National Education, Bamako, Mali, 1966–1968. 257
Final report on library affairs in Pakistan. 93
Formation archivistique à la Faculté d'information et de documentation de l'Université libanaise et organisation du dépôt de préarchivage—(mission). 53
Formation archivistique: création d'un centre de formation des archivistes, des bibliothécaires et des documentalstes: Liban—(mission) mars–avril 1974. 116
Formation artistique et formation des personnels de l'action culturelle; maisons de la culture: Algerie—(mission). 226

Title Index 141

La formation de documentalistes, de bibliothécaires et d'archivistes: Tunisie—(mission). 315

La formation de documentalistes, de bibliothécaires et l'information (IPSI): Tunisie—(mission). 316

La formation des archivistes: propositions pour un programme d'enseignement à l'École des sciences de l'information de Rabat: Maroc—(mission) 6–19 décembre 1976. 75

La formation des archivistes: propositions pour un programme d'enseignement à l'école des sciences de l'information de Rabat (ESI): Maroc—(mission) 6–19 décembre 1976. 74

La formation des bibliothécaires et le développement des bibliothèques universitaires en Afrique: pays francophones—(mission). 46

La formation et le perfectionnement de spécialistes de l'information documentaire: Répulique populaire du Bénin—(mission). 188

Future development of the University of Qatar—(mission) 5–16 January 1978. Findings and recommendations. 16 March 1978. 117

General analysis of national and provincial requirements concerning educational management information systems: Pakistan—(mission). 330

Gestion de l'éducation nationale: République populaire du Bénin—(mission) 16 novembre–1er décembre 1976. 331

(Guidelines for developing a good Engineering School Library at Polytechnic). 145

Gulf Vision System, Riyadh; a summary of the study on the feasibility of establishing a unit for the documentation on television information and programmes within the Gulf Vision System in Riyadh. 141

Historical survey of libraries in Libya up to the present time: report to Unesco. 118

Hydrogeological education and training at the University of Jordan to benefit national water resources development programmes: Hashemite Kingdom of Jordan—(mission) 6 November–5 December 1976. 300

Identification of training requirements for computerized information services: Iraq—(mission). 206

Indonesia: library development in Indonesia. 91

Indonesian national health science library, documentation center and network plan. 146

Information base for national R and D planning; Indonesia—(mission). 246

Information needs and uses in Egypt. 280

The information system of the Arab States Broadcasting Union: League of Arab States—(mission). 196

Informatisation de l'inventaire du potentiel scientifique et technique: Maroc—(mission). 121

L'Institut culturel africain; Centre regional d'etudes, de recherche et de documentation sur le développement culturel: Regional—(mission) 6 septembre–1er octobre 1976. 336

Instructional materials project in Libya: end of tour reports. 106

Integrated Rural Information System: a preliminary report on the organization of libraries and information network in Pakistan. 15

The internal system of the Documentation and Information Centre of the Arab League—(mission). 197

Introduction of machine-readable cataloguing at the National Informatin and Documentation Centre: Arab Republic of Egypt—(mission) 29 December 1976–26 January 1977. 317

Inventaire du potentiel scientifique et technologique (PST) de la Communauté Afrique—(mission). 207

Investigatory mission to Abu Dhabi in respect of the establishment of an audio-visual centre; United Arab

Title Index

Emirates—(mission) 23 July–3 August 1974. 30
Irak: organisation des archives, fevrier–avril 1970. 244
Iraq: education for library science and documentation, 28 January to 27 July 1968. 295
Iraq: library training and special libraries, November 1969–May 1970. 296
The Kabul University Library; an evaluation of its present status and recommendations for its growth and development, together with proposals for the improvement of other libraries in Kabul. 88
The Kabul University Library: terminal report. 321
Liban: Centre national de documentation pour le développement, 10 juillet–13 août 1968. 66
Liban: développement des bibliothèques, 15 novembre 1967–31 décembre 1968. 324
Liban: évaluation et developpement des bibliothèques (novembre–decembre 1964). 202
Libraries and bibliographical services: assessment report. 109
Libraries development program in Indonesia: end of tour reports. 140
Libraries in British West Africa; a report of a survey for the Carnegie Corporation of New York. October–November, 1957. 193
Libraries: Nigeria, Gold Coast, Sierra Leone and Gambia. 329
Library consultant program report to ATENE: Lebanon and U.A.R. 186
Library development in the Gambia—report to the British Council. 108
Library development (NATIS): Republic of Afghanistan—(mission) 4 July–3 August 1976. 101
'Library development plans for Gondi Shahpoor University'. 201
Library education in Hacettepa University: Turkey—(mission) 18 November–13 December 1976. 120
Library mission to Kuwait. 305

Library serivces for the visually handicapped: Malaysia—(mission). 38
Libya: organization of photographic and film archives, December 1967–May 1968. 62
The Libyan library development plan: a special report for the Ministry of Education and Guidance, Tripoli, Libyan Arab Republic. 282
Mali: réorganisation des archives, novembre–decembre 1969. 33
Manpower development for Egyptian STI services. 292
Manpower development for the University: People's Democratic Republic of Yemen—(mission). 298
Marine Sciences Centre, Lattakia: Syrian Arab Republic—(mission) 6–16 May 1978. 124
Maroc: préservation et classification des archives, novembre 1968–fevrier 1969. 245
Mauritanie: organisation de la bibliothèque nationale Mauritanie, Nouakchott (Septembre 1964–février 1965). 160
Mechanization of the national library catalogues: Egypt—(mission) October–November 1974. 175
(Memorandum on new building planning for the National Library, Teheran). 147
Mise en route du service national d'archives dans le cadre du système national d'information (NATIS): Haute-Volta—(mission) 21 février–6 mars 1976. 318
Mise sur pied d'un service national d'archives et de pré-archivage: Liban—(mission) mai–juin 1974. 14
Mission to Somalia, 30 March–1 April 1976. 200
National Documentation Centre: Sudan—(mission). Project findings and recommendations. 219
National Library of Iraq—Baghdad—(mission). 178
National library system: Somalia—(mission). Project findings and recommendations. 220

National STI system of Egypt: implementation. 293
National urban policy study informatin system; system manual and general guidelines for integration into broader information systems. 251
National resources information system: Indonesia—(mission). 278
Network of scientific informatin and documentation: Indonesia—(mission). Project findings and recommendations. 225
Organisation commune Africaine, Malagache et Mauricienne: reorganisation du service de documentation, archives et bibliogheque (suite), avril–mai 1974. 225
Organisation de la Bibliothèque nationale de Mauritanie à Nouakchott—(deuxième mission) février–Juillet 1971. 161
Organisation des Archives nationales et d'un système de préarchivage (records management): République unie du Cameroun—(mission) janvier–février 1973. 283
Organisation des services d'information pour ALDOC: Ligue des États Arabes—(mission). 9
Organisation et formation des personnels en service dans le domaine de le documentation au Ministère des enseignements primaire et secondaire et dans les orgnismes sous tutelle: Algérie—(mission) août 1971. 112
L'Organisation micrographique des dossiers au Centre de documentation nationale, Tunis: Tunisie—(mission). 242
Outline for a national documentation and information centre: United Arab Emirates—(mission) 15 December 1974–2 January 1975. 155
Outline of the Arab League Information System—(mission). 198
The Pahlavi National Library of the future: a summary of its origin, its planning, its objectives and its services. 289

Pakistan National Science Libraries and Information Centres (July–August 1966) and recruitment and training of personnel (September 1966). 158
Perfectionnement d'un service de documentation et d'études à l'Assemblée Nationale du Cameroon—(mission) 10 novembre–18 décembre 1974. 50
Pilot project for the development of a university library network: Republic of Indonesia–(mission). 301
Pilot project on the development of a library network: Malaysia—(mission) 15 April–5 June 1976. 302
Plan d'ensemble pour la création d'une école des sciences de l'information: Maroc—(mission) novembre 1973–janvier 1974. 290
Plan for a documentation centre for the Ministry of Education: State of Bahrain—(mission 14 November–1 December 1976. 13
Planification de la recherche écologique: République du Niger—(mission). 203
Planification de l'éducation et de l'information: Algérie—(mission) janvier 1969–octobre 1971. 214
Planification scientifique et technologique—(mission) 1–11 mai 1977. 250
Planning and documentation assistance assignment in Djakarta, January 14–February 7, 1968. 29
Planning and equipment of the national archives building: Malaysia—(mission) November 1971. 89
Planning and evaluating information and study functions for the Niamey Productivity Project. 63
Politique scientifique et technologique-bases de données informatisées: Sénégal—(mission) janvier 1975–octobre 1977. 122
Possibility of an Arab League Information System: League of Arab States—(mission). 267
Pour une politique nationale de

Title Index

l'informatique: Gabon—(mission). 133

Preliminary and cursory observations on law library needs in Africa. 42

Preliminary discussions for the installation of a microfilm system for the Ministry of Foreign Affairs: Saudi Arabia—(mission). 79

Preservation of materials at the National Library, Cairo—(mission) 24 November–8 December 1974. 230

A program for library development in Turkey. 306

Programme de formation en sciences et techniques de l'information de l'Université nationale: République populaire du Bénin—(mission). 189

Project pilote pour la mécanisation des services de documentation dans les pays arabes (études preliminaire): Tunisie—(mission) 18 novembre 1975–15 janvier 1976. 311

Promotion du livre: République du Mali—(mission). 129

Proposal for establishing the Department of Information and Library Services at Kuwait University. 22

Proposal for Pahlavi University Library building consultation. 148

Proposals for library development in the Hashemite Kingdom of Jordan'. 240

Proposed national information policy of Egypt. 5

Proposition pour l'organisation de la documentation en Tunisie—(mission) 4–17 décembre 1972. 18

Propositions pour la sauvegarde des manuscrits du Maroc, et en particulier de ceux de la Bibliothèque Qaraouiyine, à Fès—(mission). 284

Propositions pour le développement de l'infrastructure des bibliothéques: Tunisie—(mission) août–septembre 1974. 252

Propositions pour le développement des services de bibliothéques et de documentation en Haute-Volta —(mission) 8–17 mars 1976. 263

A publication survey trip to West Africa, Tunisia, France and Belgium. 338

Rapport de mission en République Arabe du Yemen effectuée en vue d'établir un inventaire des ressources et des reconnaissance et à l'affirmation d'identité culturelle dans ce pays. 104

Reconstitution des archives administratives—developpement d'un système national: Liban—(mission) 2–14 mai 1977. 76

A regional centre for scientific and technological information transfer: Iran—(mission) September 1977. 268

Regional documentation centre on visual and performing arts: Indonesia—(mission) 13 June–13 July 1976. 170

Renforcement de la Bibliothèque nationale: Mauritanie—(mission). Résultats et recommendations du project. 162

Réorganisation des archives nationales: Gabon—(mission) novembre–décembre 1972. 234

Réorganisation des archives nationales: République Islamique de Mauritanie—(mission) 25 février–25 mars 1976. 135

Réorganisation et développement des archives: Haute-Volta—(mission) octobre 1972. 320

Reorganization of the National Book Centre: (Bangladesh—(mission). 3

Report and proposals on the establishment and improvement of libraries and library services in Pakistan. 183

Report and survey on library services in the Sudan (1960). 286

Report of mission of the National Center for Health Statistics to Cairo, Egypt. 334

Report of survey mission to Mali. 194

Report on a mission to some of the Arab States. 179

Title Index 145

Report on a survey and recommendations for the establishment of a national library for Indonesia. 92
Report on law librarian's visit to Kabul, Afghanistan. 36
Report on library needs in British West Africa. 105
Report on literature search, documentation and related information on Mauritania. 159
Report on Pakistan's information transfer system, June 16–July 13, 1974. 87
Report on school library service of Ministry of Education. 43
Report on the development of national documentation and information services in Indonesia. 144
Report on the Egyptian state information service's mass media campaign to support population and family planning. 272
Report on the Library, Middle East Technical University, Ankara, Turkey, July 1959 to June 1960, submitted to Unesco and Middle East Technical University. 258
Report on work at the Punjab University Library, October 1915 to July 1916. 83
Report to Chancellor Torab Mehra covering recommendations for the development of Jundi Shapur University library services. 149
Report to King Abdulaziz University on library services. 19
Report to the United States Agency for International Development on audiovisual programs of library development at the Middle East Technical University, Ankara, Turkey. 322
République populaire du Bénin: politique culturelle. 102
Revue technique des activités ayant a l'informatisation de la gestion réalisées dans le cadre du 3ème project éducation financé par la Banque Mondiale: Royaume du Maroc—(mission). 322
(School library program in Libya)—end of tour report. 23
Science and technology planning: Bangladesh—(mission) 22 June–13 July 1974. 176
Science and technology policy: Jordan—(mission). 264
Science and technology policy, planning and management in the Sudan—(mission). 24
Science policy and planning of research: Iran—(mission) March 1972. 52
Science, technology and development: Iraq—(mission) 27 August–13 October 1975. 247
Scientific and technical information services: Indonesia—(mission) July 1973. 217
Scientific documentation centre: Iraq—(mission) February–April 1972. 156
Section des documentalistes, écoles des bibliothécaires, archivistes et documentalistes, de l'Université de Dakar: Sénégal—(mission) février–mars 1975. Résutats et recommendations du project. 212
Selection of a microform system for the Ministry of Foreign Affairs of the Kingdom of Saudi Arabia—(mission). 80
Sénégal: developpement des bibliothèques (octobre 1964–juin 1966). 325
Sierra Leone: book development report. 143
Sierra Leone: organization of national archives, January 1966. 34
Situation and needs of national information systems in science and technology: East Africa—(mission) 29 October–20 December 1974. 253
Situation et perspectives de l'information scientifique et technique: Syrie —(mission février–mars 1976. 90
Somalia: library development—(mission) 1963. 265
Specification for a feasibility study for the establishment of an Arab data network for information inter-

change: Federation of Arab Scientific Research Councils—(mission). 224
Study of the feasibility of using MARC tapes for co-operative processing: Malaysia—(mission). 205
Study of the present and projected activities of the Centre for Educational Research and Development, operated by the Labanese Ministry of Education: Lebanon—(mission). 35
Suggested guidelines for improving the livestock marketing information service of Mali. 209
Suggestions for organizing a library in the Ministry of Economics Export Development Department. 150
Suggestions for organizing and developing the University of Teheran Institute of Co-operative Research and Studies Library. 151
Survey of scientific and technological information resources in selected Egyptian organizations. 294
Système national d'information camerounais (SYNAICAM)—(mission) 23 février–13 mars 1976. 111
Teheran Book Processing Centre (TEBROC) proposal draft. 152
Telecommunication services for the transfer of information and data: Indonesia—(mission). 32
A teledocumentation system for the National Information and Documentation Centre: Arab Republic of Egypt—(mission) 3–30 April 1977. 269
A teledocumentation system for the National Information and Documentation Centre: Arab Republic of Egypt—(mission) 3–30 April 1977. 270
A tentative report on the University of Tehran Library. 165
Training course on book design and illustration: the Islamic Republic of Pakistan—(mission). 142
Training of Egyptian information specialists: a multifaceted system approach, final report. 136

Tripartite project review (SAU/79/002) and general analysis of information needs and priorities in higher education with a view to establishing the framework for a co-ordinated university information system: Kingdom of Saudi Arabia—(mission). 333
Tunisie: développement des bibliothèques. 61
Turkey: plans for a central general library at the Middle East Technical University. 187
United Arab Republic: a mechanized information retrieval system for the Documentation Centre in Cairo, July–September 1968. 190
United Arab Republic: proposed national press for scientific productions, March 1965. 185
University instructional materials project; feasibility study. 310
University instructional materials project; inputs on library development, concepts paper. 137
University instructional materials project; library science consultant services. 119
University library development in Indonesia: a report to the Ministry of Education and Culture, Republic of Indonesia. 327
The University of Gezira Library: a planning report. 215
University of Minia co-ordinated libraries and user services and library education programs; a planning report. 233
University of Qatar new buildings—(mission). 1
University of Wyoming Afghanistan contract with the Agency for International Development—final report 1973. 17
University textbook program component of the university instructional materials and libraries project; final report and concept paper. 65
Various memoranda and documents for development of various types of libraries and library services at the University of Teheran. 153